WITH JUST
ONE PUSH:
A New Mother's Journey of Love, Loss, and Survival

BY
LORI DENTE

Inspired By Sofia Isabella Dente

ISBN: 1490906800

ISBN 13: 9781490906805

With Just One Push

A New Mother's Journey of Love, Loss, and Survival

Lori Dente

Inspired By Sofia Isabella Dente

DEDICATIONS:

For Sofia, you changed my whole heart. You have deepened my understanding of love and have given me an unmatched appreciation for life. Thank you for giving me the gift of being your mother. Thank you for teaching me the truest meaning of maternal love.

For Alex, may you forever celebrate your sister's place in our family. May the story of her life always ignite a sense of love within you. Thank you for helping me find color in the world again and for teaching me maternal hope.

For Michael, my rock. Thank you for saving me, many times, from the depths of myself, and for offering me a perspective of beauty and love. Thank you for being the best father to our children.

Special Thanks:

To my team at Create Space...For helping this novice writer bring this book to life.

To Brandan Baki...For the countless hours you spent editing my manuscript. Thank you for offering your advice and insights, while regarding our story with such integrity and care.

To Ted Stevens...For capturing the most beautiful of pictures, that we will treasure forever, and giving us the gift of being able to soak up her beauty every day.

To my mother...Thank you for believing in me and in Sofie's legacy, and for enabling me to continue to share her life in this way.

To all of my family and friends...Thank you for your unending support and love throughout this journey of life. Thank you for your willingness to sit with us in our darkest days, and for continuing to sit with us as each uncertain day draws near. You have been my confidants, my protectors, my strength, and my hope. Thank you for blindly supporting me and holding me up on my weakest of days, but most importantly, I thank you endlessly for loving Sofie so much.

CHAPTER 1

A BEGINNING FULL OF HOPE AND PROMISE...

I always promised my beautiful baby that we would write a book together while I was on maternity leave. I know what you're thinking...*She's clearly a first-time mom. How else could you possibly explain the naivety of imagining such a task?* I can almost hear the playful jeering now. "Good luck with that one! (Insert boisterous laughter here.) Yeah, you write your book, right between feedings, naps, diaper changes, laundry, and a screaming newborn. She clearly has no clue what she's in for." And man was that last person right. I had absolutely no idea what was in store for me.

The book was supposed to be a fun and breezy read, a humorous, sassy look at pregnancy. I even had the title picked out: *Does This Baby Make My Belly Look Fat?!* Yup, I was one of those pregnant people who loved every last minute of the experience. I was one of *those* pregnant women that other pregnant women envied. I never had even an ounce of morning sickness, I never felt any more tired than typical, I had no swollen ankles or disgusting stretch marks. I never even had weird cravings that sent my husband to the grocery story in the middle of the night. It didn't really bother me much to get up to use the bathroom a couple of times a night. Even the labor was so much better than it had been described by every other woman I know. Pregnancy...I

1

could do pregnancy and did it pretty well if you ask me, all while wearing three-inch heels!

I promised my sweet baby that we'd write a book while I was on maternity leave; I just never could have imagined it would be this kind of a book.

Since you are about to so willingly embark on a very personal journey with me, let me begin by telling you a bit about myself. I am thirty-three years old. I have been married for three years. My husband, Mike, and I have two dogs, Fenway and Reagan, and we live in the house where he grew up in a friendly community in Ohio. I moved here eight years ago, trading the fast-paced city life of Washington, DC, for the small-town warmth of Copley, Ohio. I know what you're thinking: most normal people would be eager to leave the Midwest for the big, bright lights of city life.

But for me, the decision was simple. I have one sister, Lisa, who is just two years older than me. We talk every day, even during those catty sisterly moments. The only time we separated was when she attended graduate school in Boston, and I attended graduate school in DC. The separation felt daunting at first, but we maintained our closeness.

She had relocated from Boston to Ohio just after she got married, and the moment I learned I was about to become an aunt for the first time, my mind was made up. I had finished my master's degree in social work, and while I loved my job and friends, I knew I didn't want to be a long-distance aunt.

I packed my DC life up and made the trek to the Midwest, where I was able to watch my niece grow up and soon another niece and then a nephew. I never doubted that I made the right choice. Family is what matters most to me.

I was incredibly blessed to quickly find a job as a pediatric intensive care social worker at a free-standing local children's hospital. I have the opportunity to work with patients and families as they face uncertain and occasionally incredibly tragic times. Friends and family members often say to me, "You seriously have the worst job in the world."

Undeniably it can be difficult. No one wants to see children sick, injured, or worse…dying. But I always feel honored to be welcomed to sit in the presence of a family during such a vulnerable time in their lives and offer any support or comfort I possibly can. It is an intimate experience that is difficult to explain, but I have always felt called in this way and am humbled to offer what I can during such pain and tragedy. And of course, the children who I see do well and who I help get home with their families—well, that fuels the hope that brings me to work every day. Those moments help bring light to the darker ones.

My husband, Mike, and I couldn't be more different in some ways. We are kind of an oxymoron as a couple—a case of extreme opposites in some areas and intense similarities in others. I think that's what makes us work so well.

Mike is six years older than me. He works as a compensation manager with human resources in the corporate world. I would love to describe his work in more detail for you, but the truth is I don't really understand it.

He works in numbers; I work with emotion. We bring a very different set of skills to our relationship.

Of the two of us, Mike is the introvert. He is logical, analytical, and always thought-filled. He is strong in his faith and values life, love, honesty, and ethics. While I, on the other hand, am a flaming extrovert, a chronic cheerleader personality through life, probably ad nauseam, who always tries to elicit a good laugh from the crowd.

The value of family is where we form common ground. While he is quiet to most outsiders, Mike's values speak loudly to those who know him. His family is crucial to him. At just about thirty years old, he gave up his home, some career aspirations, and an abundance of time to move in with his mother, who was suffering with severe Alzheimer's disease. His father passed away after a long illness when Mike was just fifteen, so he is no stranger to the caregiving role. He took care of his mother willingly until she passed away just before we met in 2006.

Mike and his twin brother are the youngest of six children, Mike coming in older by just one minute. Despite his place among his siblings, he's never one to ask for help. In fact, most of his siblings see him as the rock and often seek him out for clarity.

Mike and I began our relationship as a result of a blind date courtesy of my sister-in-law, Cathy. Cathy and I work together in the social work department at the local children's hospital. She is our department secretary. It didn't take long after she started for us to develop a close bond. Cathy is ten years older than Mike and a proud big sister. She is also in the flaming extrovert category, and I was immediately drawn to her zest for life, sense of humor, and incredible warmth. As our bond grew, I recall learning one day that Cathy had a daughter, Jamie, who had passed away at just age eleven. I was always mystified by this. Cathy is so joy filled on even the most ordinary of days. She greets every moment with an unmatched enthusiasm and I just couldn't fathom that she had experienced such sorrow in her life. That very enthusiasm is what I love about her.

Being the proud big sister, Cathy wasted little time in trying to set up Mike and me. One quality Cathy has is perseverance as it took a good year before we finally gave in, mostly to stifle the constant nagging. It didn't take long for us to understand why she had been nagging so loudly. We were just too stubborn to realize that she recognized our compatibility long before we had ever met.

Not much time passed before we were engaged and married, and life was wonderful. We had married later in life, so we felt like we were in a good place to expand our family.

We had difficulty conceiving at first. I had my first appointment with a fertility specialist in January of 2010. I hated having to be there. I felt so broken. It was an overwhelming process as we learned of potential options, none of which I was sure I wanted.

I sat in the doctor's office on the cold, hard table, waiting for the doctor to come in and do his first exam. What happened next, I'll never forget.

"Ms. Dente?"

"Yes," I said nervously.

"I'm not going to do an exam on you today."

"Oh, OK." I didn't really understand the full process of this clinic, so my quizzical face must have been apparent.

He smiled brilliantly as he offered his explanation. "I'm not doing an exam today because you're pregnant."

I looked at him wide-eyed, laughed, and shook…a lot. I playfully exclaimed, "Wow, you guys *are* good!"

I went back to work and excitedly pondered the perfect way to announce the news to Mike. Being an eternal optimist, months earlier I had ordered a tiny Boston Red Sox jersey because we are both big fans. I wrapped it up and placed it unnoticeably underneath some paper and a simple card. The message on the card was a touching letter that appeared to be from me but was revealed at the end to be from our unborn baby.

I watched his face soften as he read the words from his growing child: "I am excited to imagine the rest of our lives together. I wriggle with joy every time I hear your laugh. As I continue to grow, I wonder if I will learn to have your strength, your knowledge, and your sense of integrity. I love you so much already and know that will only continue to grow. I can't wait to meet you in September. Love, your growing baby."

The moment was magnificent. He shared my joy for our upcoming new role as parents. The next night when he came home from the gym, I was lying in bed. He put his ear to my belly and playfully said, "I can hear the heartbeat." *What a goofball*, I thought. *He clearly doesn't know that you can't even hear the heartbeat by ultrasound until eight weeks.* I loved him for his excitement.

Little did I know we wouldn't get that chance. The next morning, just two days after we learned of our joyous news, I miscarried. I sobbed every time I went to the bathroom that day, literally watching our hopes and dreams go down the drain. It was amazing to me how attached you can get to the idea of someone in such a short time. As quickly as we had learned of the pregnancy, it was over.

We continued to try to conceive but were unsuccessful. We were starting to feel pressured by our doctors and ourselves, so we decided to take a break from some medicines and from plotting out the timing of our attempts. We took a break from the stress of it all. We had a big trip to Italy planned in mid-May and thought when we returned we could talk more about how we wanted to proceed.

About five days before we left for Italy I decided to take a pregnancy test before going out with some friends. Just in case, I didn't want to even have a sip of wine. We hadn't planned our trying that month and had ceased all medicines to assist the process, but I wanted to be safe.

It was a Friday morning at 6:30 right before work. I took a pregnancy test, and much to my surprise, it was positive.

Throughout our months of trying, I had wondered how I would top my first proclamation of pregnancy to Mike. It didn't go like this at all in my head, but alas, this is how it happened…

I walked downstairs in my robe with my giant, frizzy, crazy, curly hair sticking up every which way. Shaking, I shoved my hand with the pee-coated stick in front of his face and said, "Does this look positive to you?"

He replied with a, "Yup."

I said, "Well OK then. I'm going to get in the shower."

That was it. We were simply in shock, but our news was confirmed later that day by my physician, and my lab work looked wonderful.

We had frequent appointments in the beginning that included an ultrasound every two weeks, which was fine with me because that meant I got to see my growing baby a lot. We saw the heartbeat at six weeks and heard it at eight, and ultrasound after ultrasound image displayed a healthy, growing baby. We stopped having such regular ultrasounds at week twelve, and it wasn't until week twenty that I got to see my baby again. The complete ultrasound at week twenty was amazing. It revealed a perfectly healthy, developing, beautiful (and might I add a little bit sassy) baby girl!

I was elated. She was the first girl on my husband's side in nine years! We had picked out names when we were in Italy, and our girl name was my favorite. Her daddy picked it, and it was beautiful. It was Sofia Isabella, and we would call her Sofie.

And Sofie she became, from that moment forward. We always referred to her by name. We had friends question, "What if when she comes out, she doesn't look like a Sofie? What if you change your mind?" That was nonsense to me; she *was* Sofie, our precious, loved baby girl.

I remember rushing out after that appointment and buying her the first of many, many beautiful baby girl clothes. My favorite piece quickly became a navy blue sweater dress adorned with red argyle hearts. It was full price, which goes against everything I believe in, but she just *had* to have it.

When I got home and excitedly displayed her new outfits for Mike, he looked at that sweater dress and then raised his eyebrows at me with that "Seriously?" look on his face. I playfully explained, "She *needed* to have it."

"A sweater dress for a newborn?" he taunted.

"Yes!" I said adamantly. "It will be her Valentine's Day dress!"

And she did get to wear that dress on Valentine's Day. It just wasn't at all how we had planned.

To say that I bonded with Sofie in utero is an understatement. I talked to her constantly. I knew her every move, kick, roll, and turn before it happened. She and I would playfully banter with the, "I push and you kick back" games. I would feel her move with excitement when certain songs came on the radio that I determined were her favorites. Very quickly, everything I did was for Sofie, and I loved every second of it.

Even my baby shower was all for her. I refused to let it be a celebration of me in any way. It had to be all about her, and it was. I made a feminine cake in bubblegum pink, decorated with a quilted and pearled design on the icing, and topped it off with a delicately pearled S just for her. Her beautiful twenty-week ultrasound picture was proudly displayed by its side, which highlighted her profile and her perfect button nose. It was her party. I was just her vessel.

The pregnancy flew by until I hit thirty-five weeks. Then it came to a very slow crawl. We had a minor hiccup in the pregnancy that bought me a few days of bed rest and a lot of anxiety. I woke one morning, waiting for Sofie to begin her typical morning utero acrobatics, only to notice she wasn't as active. She was moving but not in typical Sofie fashion. I decided to head to the doctor's office out of precaution. Mike was working from home that day and offered to come with me. It seemed unnecessary. I was certain they would check her, all would be fine, and I would be on my way to work in no time. I would simply call him when I was finished.

On my arrival, they hooked me up to a monitor to check her heart rate, and while they assured me everything appeared to be fine, they decided to do an ultrasound to help ease my anxiety that something seemed off. The ultrasound didn't alleviate any anxiety but rather increased everyone else's in the room. The ultrasound revealed that somehow, Sofie was compressing her umbilical cord, decreasing her oxygen intake and causing her heartbeat to drop from the 150s to 54. Every doctor in the practice rushed into that tiny, dark ultrasound room. They were all shouting.

"Call 911!"

"Call the hospital and tell them she's on her way!"

"It's her heart!"

"This baby needs to come out now!"

They began yelling commands at me for what seemed like an eternity.

"Flip to your side!" I could barely breathe or make out their words through my sobbing tears. What was happening?! Was my baby girl OK? Did she have a heart defect that was missed? Why were we calling 911!?

My incoherent thoughts were sharply interrupted when one of the doctors yelled, "Her heart rate is coming back up, and she is breathing fine."

He explained to me that he believed Sofie had compressed her umbilical cord, cutting off her oxygen supply and causing the deceleration in her heart rate.

"It happens more than you think," he said. "It is just rare to catch it on an ultrasound."

They permitted me to drive myself to the hospital for further monitoring. Mike met me there, as did my following OBGYN, who happened to be on call that day. She is a tiny woman; petite doesn't do her justice. She is kind and compassionate. I had been a patient of hers for eight years. She understood my tears and assured me that everything was fine once again. They kept me for three days to ensure there were no further drops in her heart rate, and thankfully, there were none. Still my anxiety continued to heighten with each passing day. I wanted to make sure Sofie was safe, plus I couldn't wait to meet this little girl. I pleaded with her daily to make her entrance at any time once we hit the full-term stage. But my pleading didn't work.

Sofie's due date came and went despite all of my excessive walking, eating spicy foods, etc. The plan from my doctor was to induce me nine days past my due date if she didn't make her arrival before then. It felt like an eternity, and given the events that occurred at thirty-five weeks, it felt unsafe. Sofie was bigger now and running out of room. I didn't want to chance her compressing her umbilical cord again. Paranoia was beginning to take over. I had planned to beg my doctor at my next appointment, four days past Sofie's due date, to please induce sooner. My plan to plead with my doctor was unnecessary; we never made it there.

Instead, on Tuesday, three days past due, I woke up again feeling like something seemed off with Sofie. I called the doctor two times that morning, and they finally had me come to the office in the early afternoon. Sofie's heart rate was strong and steady, and I was having a lot of contractions. They ordered an ultrasound, which showed a wide-eyed Sofie breathing but not moving. The doctor said she wasn't convinced I wasn't in labor, and off I went to the hospital. My OB gave an order to induce me since I was already past due…and the process began. We were finally about to meet my beautiful baby girl.

The labor was not as bad as I expected. I mean it hurt, and I got sick a little, but I had expected much worse. I had an unusually quick first-time labor, and my cervix dilated from two to ten centimeters in just a couple of hours.

The labor room was a blast; we were texting and updating everyone every step of the way. We had visitors and had the best labor and delivery nurses you could ask for. The room itself felt joyous and had a sunny disposition. It was the perfect start to the best birthday party celebration you could imagine!

The labor continued. They broke my water, checked my cervix, and announced that it was time to push. I quickly texted everyone I knew while the medical staff was preparing. "I am about to push!" I felt like the whole world was holding their breath with me. We are about to become a family of three and meet this baby girl who had already changed my whole life.

I ended up having to push for a couple of hours, which was fatiguing. Throughout the process, I kept hearing a blending of voices—the nurses', the doctor's, Mike's, Cathy's, my fifteen-year-old niece Lizzy's, and my sister, Lisa's, who were all in the room cheering me on.

"Keep going!"

"You are doing great!"

"Just one more push!"

And finally, with just one push, I felt my baby girl enter the world, and our world was completely changed.

CHAPTER 2

THE CRASHING SILENCE...

The room was so dark to me. I can still remember it. It was 12:15 a.m., and the only source of light was coming from the overhead spotlight, which had been pulled down closely for the doctors. The light was so blinding that it distorted everything I could see into darkness.

I remember feeling Sofie leave my body and enter the world. For the first time throughout the labor, I felt myself let go of anxiety and concern and give in to the joy of meeting her. I had been so cautious throughout the process, questioning every medical person who entered the room, "Does she look OK? How is Sofie doing? Are you sure she is OK?" I was constantly reassured. I told everyone that I would relax once she was safely out, I could hear her crying, and I was told that she was just fine.

As I mentioned, paranoia had set in after that incident at thirty-five weeks. Even on that Tuesday morning, all of this began with me once again feeling as if something wasn't right. No one else appeared concerned throughout the labor and delivery process, but I never felt convinced. Not until I could hear her cry and was handed my baby would I rest assured.

Sofie had made her arrival into this highly anticipating world. There we were in the delivery room, waiting to hold our precious newborn.

I was now completely blinded by this bright light of darkness and the crashing silence that followed. I was prepared initially for some of the silence. They were not going to allow Sofie to cry right away because they had found meconium in my broken water. Meconium is the product of the first bowel movements in infants. They should not occur until after the baby is out of the womb, but occasionally meconium can occur during labor or if the baby has experienced something to cause them stress in utero. The reason for the silence was to ensure that she didn't breathe any of it in. There was a special team on standby right by my bed. I was worried but was again reassured that this can be common during labor.

Upon her final push into the world, my eyes filled with joyous tears, but it didn't take long for me to notice that everything in the room had changed. Laughter turned to solemnity, smiles turned into concern, color flushed out of everyone's faces…Sofie wasn't breathing.

Sofie was whisked to the isolette on the side of my bed and was swarmed by a hive of quick-moving medical staff, all of them blocking my view.

"Is she OK?" I kept asking, but nobody answered. I finally looked directly at my sister and asked her. She mechanically shook her head yes, but I knew she was lying.

I could hear bits and pieces of frantic medical conversations as I stared at Mike's serious face, his eyes glued to his daughter the entire time.

"She has a lot of meconium in her lungs."

"My God it is caked in there."

"I need to drop an NG tube."

"OK, it's mostly clear."

"She can cry now."

"We need her to cry."

"Why isn't she crying?" The words were spoken louder.

"She's not breathing."

"I need to bag her. Get me an ET tube."

It was horrifying. I laid there staring into the blinding, dark light and sobbed. Working in the pediatric intensive care unit for almost eight years, I had come to pick up a lot of medical knowledge. I understood all of these terms; none of them were anything that you want to hear describing your newborn baby girl.

What had just happened? Everything was fine. Everyone told me she was fine.

We were told that she had aspirated some of the meconium into her lungs and she needed a ventilator for a little while because her lungs were sick, likely due to an infection from the meconium. We were assured that babies recover well from this, but she would need to be transported next door to the very children's hospital where I am employed. I buried my eyes in my hands and just broke down. I can't even describe the terror I felt in that moment or the amount of tears that were pouring from my eyes. It was as if every amount of security and control I had exited my body with my baby girl.

Mike continued to assure me that she would be OK.

"She just needed a little extra help," he said.

And then I uttered the words that I'll never forget. You see, I had caught a brief glimpse of Sofie between the medical bodies caring for her. I could see her trying to take breaths, and they looked abnormal to me. They looked like the breaths I had seen all too many times on children at the hospital who had suffered severe brain injuries.

I looked at Mike and said, "I'm so afraid we'll be cleaning out her nursery." Everyone in the room tried to support me, tried to tell me all of the right things that would make anyone in this situation "feel better."

Then the silence grew louder, and the already dark room somehow seemed darker. In walked a doctor I only recognized from the neonatal intensive care unit at the children's hospital. Following behind were my nurses and my delivering OB. I barely looked up, only to see that none of them would make eye contact with me. Their heads hung so low that I swear their chins could have touched the floor.

The neonatologist came close to my bed and delivered the earth-shattering words that would rock our worlds forever: "We are worried about brain damage."

There are no words in the human language to describe the primal emotions I felt upon hearing those words. I was beyond devastated. I remember not being able to look at the doctor who had just spoken; I just kept my hand over my eyes and shook my head, hoping to shake myself out of this horrifying nightmare.

Not only did I not get my baby girl thrown onto my belly after she entered the world, not only did I not get to hear her crying voice for the first time, but her first out-of-utero touches weren't tender caresses by her mama or daddy. They were rough, fast-working hands pushing tubes down her throat and into her lungs. But one of the worst realizations I had was that I hadn't even gotten to see her face. I didn't even know what my daughter looked like.

They were able to bring Sofie in for me to see her before she was taken to the next hospital. She was in this cold, sterile, hard, plastic transport isolette that looked so…medical. She had a breathing tube down her throat connected to the ventilator that was giving her breath. She was still having those abnormal breaths and jerky movements that scared me to death because I understood them all too well. I asked if I could touch her, and I was terrified as stuck my finger in to touch her soft, warm, lifeless hand.

She looked like me. Panic stricken, I yelled for them just to take her, to get her the help she needed right away, and in an instant, they were gone.

This was not the life we were supposed to be living. Someone screwed up! I remember thinking, *Get that poor baby to the hospital and bring me in my baby girl!* This just couldn't be happening. But it was.

Through my tears, I looked up and asked the doctor when I could leave to go to the hospital with Sofie. She kindly responded, "As soon as you can walk." It was the longest five hours of my life.

CHAPTER 3

DAY ONE OF LIFE: SEVENTY-TWO ICE-COLD HOURS...

I arrive at the children's hospital just five hours after giving birth, yet it seems like a lifetime. Little do I know that it has been. Our life as we knew it is gone, and we are embarking on our new life as a family of three, though that journey hasn't started out at all as we had planned.

As we are still absorbing how we got here, we understand that Sofie compressed her umbilical cord again about twenty-four hours before I had her. This time it was compressed for too long, cutting off sufficient oxygen to her brain and causing her brain damage.

Today we understand that while I slept on Monday night, my baby girl was suffocating and I didn't know. While my baby girl's brain was being injured cell by cell, while she was clinging to life, I was in a peaceful slumber. I don't know that I can ever forgive myself for that.

Mike meets me at the front door of the children's hospital, and we head toward the NICU (neonatal intensive care unit). These familiar walls that I walked just yesterday seem so different to me now. I have walked these halls countless times in eight years and at all hours of the day and night, but this morning I can barely find my way.

A dream state is the only way I can describe this experience. These halls, the people—they all have an illusion of being underwater, except Mike and I are the only ones who appear to be drowning.

The NICU is made up of several glass rooms, which each contain about four babies. There are no dividers between babies to allow the nurses to care for more than one child at a time. There is no privacy. The rooms are kept dim and quiet to prevent too much stimulation for the babies as they heal and grow.

As we near Sofie's spot in the front room of the NICU, I fear I won't even be able to recognize which baby is mine. But I do—immediately. She is so small, just seven pounds, but next to some of these tiny NICU babies, she looks giant. Her color is so much better than when I saw her just five hours ago. She is pink and perfect, adorned with just a diaper and a royal blue, ice-cold cap on her head.

It's a new treatment, we are told. It puts the brain into a hypothermic state to prevent any further brain injury. She must wear it for exactly seventy-two hours. There is a protocol manual by her crib side, instructing, down to the minute, how Sofie should be treated with this innovative intervention. We are told that we can apply gentle pressure to Sofie's hands, arms, legs, or feet, but we can't hold her, we can't stroke her, and we must keep any stimulation to a minimum.

The doctor who delivered the awful words of *brain damage* greets us somberly. He says they did a "poor man's EEG" prior to placing the cap on her head to read her brain activity and that it showed "high voltage," which is good, but there was some abnormality.

OK, I think. *We can deal with that. Maybe Sofie will have some therapy needs, maybe some swallowing issues. Maybe she'll need some programs to help her meet her milestones. We can work with that. I'm a social worker for God's sake; resources we can do.*

Her lungs have essentially recovered from the meconium. They may be able to take the breathing tube out soon. I notice her lack of movement...of life. I know from my experience just two floors up that most children are sedated on the ventilator to prevent them from yanking out their breathing tubes. Those same children will need to have that sedation lifted just before doctors remove the tube to ensure they are awake enough to breathe on their own.

I am aware of my terror as I ask, "When will her sedation be lifted in preparation for the removal of the tube?"

I feel as if I am kicked in the gut when he replies, "She isn't on any."

I know this isn't OK. Babies should be moving, kicking, grasping, sucking…but maybe she isn't doing these things because of her frozen little brain. Maybe her body is reserving itself to heal. *Oh God, I hope her body is reserving itself to heal.*

Our nurse on that first day, Laurie, would become one of Sofie's primary nurses. She is so protective of Sofie. She immediately treats her with the care and regard that any mother would want for her child. Laurie is also very protective of Mike and me. Mike will later come to refer to her as our guardian angel. She convinces us to take a break at least to get something to eat. We don't feel like eating, but Mike and I know we need to keep up our strength to be present for Sofie. And since I have just given birth and have not slept in two days, Mike convinces me to force some food down.

We walk the halls once again making our way to the cafeteria. Although we don't realize it, it is just after 8:00 a.m. The workday has begun. It takes no time for us to run into co-workers and friends. People who just saw me leave yesterday with my giant, pregnant belly now stare at me, puzzled and shocked to see me. Their support is kind, but I feel like crumbling to the ground every time someone recognizes my deflated stomach and asks me what I am doing here. We quickly retreat back to the NICU.

Word of our admission has spread like wildfire through the halls. Familiar faces start flooding our space—co-workers, friends, and acquaintances. It is difficult to process what has just happened in front of so many people.

We publically announce Sofie's arrival via social media because so many people have been expecting her arrival to occur any moment. For days we have been receiving messages via Facebook that read, "I wake up every morning and race to my computer first thing, just to see if that baby girl has been born yet."

We know we need to share what is happening, and we could certainly use any prayers for healing. I could never have imagined just how important this step in our journey would become. Hesitantly, we simply share, "Sofie is here but is in need of prayers as she is having a very difficult time." It is not at all the joy-filled birth announcement we had planned.

With that small statement, something so much larger is ignited. People spring into action for this tiny baby they have never even seen.

17

We quickly begin to receive notifications and messages from people all over the world to let us know they are keeping Sofie in their prayers. It feels powerful. I need it to be powerful.

Mike and I sit devastated at her bedside, one of us on each side of her plastic crib. Our fingers are pressed against her velvety, pink skin.

Utterly heartbroken, I whisper closely and repeatedly into her ear, "My poor, poor, sweet baby girl. I'm so sorry, Sofie. I'm so sorry Mama's body has failed you. This wasn't how it was supposed to be, I promise. I'm so, so sorry. Mama loves you, sweet pea. Please, please wake up, baby girl."

I close my eyes, put light pressure on Sofie's hand, and lower my head. "Oh God, heal her…please heal her. She doesn't deserve this. You *have* to heal her. Please heal her." My tears fall with every tick of the clock, with every breath a prayer for a miracle. Seventy-two ice-cold hours…we'll know more in seventy-two cold hours.

CHAPTER 4

DAY TWO OF LIFE: AN EMPTY STOMACH AND AN EVEN EMPTIER HEART...

The day is blurry. I wake up in the morning with every possible hope that I will be waking up at home and will tell Mike of this horrible dream. But when my eyes open, I find myself in a strange sleep room. It wasn't a dream at all. I call into the NICU about five hundred feet away to make sure Sofie is OK...well, as OK as she can be right now. She had an "uneventful night" for the few hours we were away from her. I guess that's good, but I do wish we had been woken to an excitable call yelling for us to come down right away because Sofie was awake. We didn't get that call. Uneventful certainly isn't bad if it means that Sofie had no additional difficulties, though. I'll take that for now. Besides, her brain still needs time to heal. We can give her that. We will give her that. This cool cap is supposed to be amazing...cutting edge. I sure hope so.

I go to take the fastest shower imaginable and am caught off guard by my empty stomach. I hate it. I was huge at the end of my pregnancy, full of Sofie, and I loved it. Today my empty stomach is just a precursor to my broken heart. How the hell did we get here? How the hell did this happen?

I have many more minutes of crying today than moments of strength. I don't mean to be so sad around her. I just hate that we are here. We should be learning how to change her diapers, how to feed her. We should be franticly trying to figure out her cues, learning just what she needs to help her stop crying and to find comfort.

Instead we are in this strange space. The only thing I can do for Sofie right now is make milk.

Every time I pump my milk for Sofie, I am alone. It is a dangerous place to be. I can't slow my mind from what I have witnessed in so many patients and am now witnessing in my daughter. My mind jumps to the road ahead. We have been placed on a track, and I know exactly where it leads. I don't know how to derail its path. I would throw myself on the rails if it could change the course for her.

I use this time alone to pray unceasingly for a miracle, for complete healing for my baby girl. I cry, scream, and plead with God to heal her. I hope He is listening. Today is Mike's father's birthday. He passed away many years ago, so we never got to meet. But still, I talk to him, to his wife, to my grandparents, to Sofie's young cousin, all of whom are no longer on this earth, to please heal her, to pray to God for her.

I plead desperately aloud to whoever is listening in the heavens, "Please give Mike the opportunity to be the dad he should get to be to Sofie. He loves her so much. He doesn't deserve this. Sofie certainly doesn't deserve this. Please take me instead. It should have been me who had a problem after delivery, not her! Please fix this. You can still fix this. Lord, You can still fix this. Please fix this. Please heal her!"

Mike remains so hopeful. He is so in love with his little girl, and he is so strong. He continues to give me reasons why she isn't doing any of the things she should be.

"How is she supposed to suck with that breathing tube in her mouth?" he asks, defending his helpless baby girl.

I hesitantly tell him that I have seen the newest of babies suck on their breathing tubes effortlessly with their little tongues.

He protectively responds back, "She's had hardly any food yet. She has no energy to start moving. People can't expect her to do all of this with no food in her system."

I don't want to crush his hope, but I know all too well that even despite his reasons for her inactivity, she should be doing more.

I walk back to the NICU after one of my pump 'n' prayer sessions to find Mike sitting close to Sofie's crib side, reading her a book. It is one of the most endearing moments I will ever experience in my lifetime. It doesn't take me long to recognize the cover. It is one of my favorites, *Guess How Much I Love You?* It is perfect. I sit close to them both, gently press my fingers against her soft, velvety skin, and listen to the story as my tears soak the blanket cloaking her defenseless body. For a brief second, this moment almost feels normal.

CHAPTER 5

DAY THREE OF LIFE: HOPE IN THE FORM OF A COLD CAP...

Today is much of the same. I wake up nauseated. I pump and pray throughout the day. I continue to beg and plead with God. Family and friends come to visit, and it is difficult. Many of them don't understand what is happening. Hell, I don't understand what is happening.

They bring her gifts. One gift bag that explodes with baby girl, cheerful colors contains wonderfully girly, frilly dresses, a welcome to the world present. It breaks my heart because I know she is likely not going to get to wear them.

Each morning the medical staff "rounds" on Sofie. The NICU doctor who has been caring for her a few days now continues to let us know that she is very worried.

I ask her what she means.

"Do you mean you are worried that Sofie has brain damage?" I choke out through tears. "Because I know she does. Or when you say you are worried, are you worried she is not going to survive this?"

She responds so warmly, "I think she will survive, but I am worried her brain damage is more severe than we initially thought."

Sofie is scheduled to have an EEG tomorrow to determine her brain activity. This will be read by the neurologist, the brain expert, if you will. The first doctor said he thought Sofie had mild damage. This doctor fears it is more severe. I understand this doctor's concern, but I am holding out for the brain expert.

The nurse caring for Sofie today takes her cool cap off for scheduled "head check" time to make sure there is no skin breakdown. I get to be there for the head check. They remove the cap, and her head is squiggly and indented from the cooling design of the cap itself. I begin to cry. The nurse comforts me, explaining that it is just from the edema and it will go away. That isn't why I was crying. It is the first time that I have gotten to see and touch Sofie's hair. It is her daddy's color, dark blonde. It looks curly like mine, but I think that is because of the cap. I can't believe I haven't been able to hold her and just stroke and smell her hair.

The nurse asks Mike and me if we want to save the cool cap once it is taken off for good. We joke that we'll let her know, depending on how this all turns out. I remember a couple of years ago when Mike and I went on a hot air balloon ride. I remember thinking how insane it was that we were putting so much trust into a tiny wicker basket. Today that seems trivial. I can't believe how much trust, faith, and hope we are placing in this ice-cold, freezing blue cap on her head. Heck, if it is as good as everyone says it is, we will buy stock in that company and encourage them to make pink cool caps for all the baby girls! The nurse puts up a note to save the cool cap for us. Maybe it will be a neat scrapbook opportunity one day to show Sofie just how far she came and how strong she was right from the beginning.

It is around midnight, and Sofie's cool cap will be taken off for good at three o'clock this morning. We ask if we can be present. We are encouraged to sleep, and they promise they will call us if they need us. They warn us that kids can seize when they come off of the cap. As much as I do not want to see my sweet girl seize, I also don't want her to be alone if she does. They promise they'll call me. We read Sofie *Guess How Much I Love You?*, which has quickly become our nighttime routine. Mike and I lean in, kiss her gently, and begin the long walk down the dark hallway to our room, just five hundred feet away, but it feels like we are oceans apart. This is my least favorite part of every day.

I love you, sweet pea. Stay strong, baby girl. Stay strong.

A note from Sofie's mama:

I have mentioned earlier that at the moment we shared Sofie's difficult arrival in the world of social media, something changed. Mike and I went from being in this horrific situation seemingly alone to recognizing that thousands of people were supporting all three of us throughout this fight. Through prayers, messages of love, e-mails, and cards sent to Sofie, Mike, and me at the hospital, we quickly understood that along with receiving much-welcomed support, Sofie was touching lives and changing the hearts of countless people the moment they learned of her. People who knew Mike and I became messengers for this baby girl, and like wildfire, word of Sofie's arrival, life, and love spread to thousands who we would never even meet.

During this journey, I began to write daily to the world of people who were captivated by Sofie and her story. What began as medical updates transitioned into my journey of love, loss, and survival. What you are about to continue reading are my writings in real time as I faced uncertainty in a world that became so different for Mike and me than we could ever have expected. Thank you for embarking on this journey.

CHAPTER 6

DAY FOUR OF LIFE: SEVEN POUNDS, ZERO OUNCES OF PURE HOPE...

S ofie has tolerated coming off of her cool cap as expected. We sat by her bedside this morning continuing to pray, and we can truly feel the peace that is coming from everyone else's prayers as well. Yesterday Sofie stopped breathing over the ventilator, which was concerning.

It is devastating to watch the few positive things she is doing start to fade away. I don't know what that means for her. I take a short break to pump and pray and take some gifts back to our room. I open one; it is a delicate white angel statue that simply reads "Hope." It is beautiful.

I take a minute to focus on that gift and pray. I pray for Sofie to be able to breathe on her own, knowing that breathing tube cannot stay in permanently. I know she has to be able to successfully breathe on her own to avoid some really ugly conversations that could head our way. I stare at the angel statue, my finger gently caressing the word *hope* over and over again, as if waiting for a genie to appear and grant me my three wishes. I would only need one.

When I reentered the NICU, Mike excitedly greeted me at the entrance. "Sofie began breathing again on her own again about thirty minutes ago."

Hope and a small, unsure wave of relief wash over me. Hope.

She held steady for over two hours, and the doctors were able to take her off of the ventilator. She is holding her own for the time being. She is hooked up to a twenty-four-hour EEG, which will help us gain some insight as to what type of injury she has. We can absolutely feel and tell that the prayers are working for our little girl.

The Results Are In

This morning after much uncertainty, Mike decided to go to our church for mass. It is just a couple of blocks away. I remained with Sofie. I will certainly continue to pray for her, but I cannot get myself to leave her bedside for very long. I walk alone toward the NICU carrying some books to read her, my personal belongings, and some milk for Sof. I immediately see the neurologist sitting at the nurse's station. An enormous wave of nausea overwhelms me.

I do not make eye contact. I dart for her crib side and text Mike that the doctor is nearby. But before I have even emptied my arms of all of my things, the neurologist is by my side. He says the EEG tells them that Sofie isn't seizing, and that is good news.

He looks as if he is about to walk away, and my voice wavers as I feebly ask him further about the results of her EEG. His words pierce my entire heart when he solemnly shares it is, "Low to flat everywhere."

I feel my legs start to tremble underneath me, and my wounded heart shatters as I am encompassed in tears. Our NICU doctor rushes to my side to comfort me. She is so gentle with my fragile self and softly asks me where Mike is. I quip with a sarcastic irony, "He is at church." I fall into her tiny, petite frame and sob. I muster the strength to remain upright, and I convince her that I am OK enough to walk back to the waiting room to call Mike.

I dial his number, and he answers. I can barely speak through my tears as I deliver the heartbreaking news.

Mike is back within minutes. He is also able to speak with the neurologist. The news hurts just as bad the second time around. I have never felt so helpless. For months I planned for her. I read, researched, and prepared to take care of her every need. Yet now I can't help her at all.

Out of all of the heartache of the day a glimmer of pure joy peeks through. We are able to hold Sofie for the first time. I let Mike go first.

I nearly sit on his lap as he holds her. I feel like a child at her birthday party staring at a table filled with presents who was told she has to wait to open them.

When it is my turn, it feels as if Sofie just melts into me. Her skin is so warm, and even though it is the first time I'm holding her in this outside world, she feels completely familiar to my arms. I feel like we are one again. I wish I could put her back inside of my womb, to keep her safe from this terrible world. Holding her is the only time my heart feels whole again.

This journey into parenthood is not at all what we had expected, and no pregnancy guides have prepared us for what lies ahead.

CHAPTER 7

DAY FIVE OF LIFE: A SETBACK…AND SOME SMALL SIGNS OF HOPE…

Sofie had a difficult day today. She was working incredibly hard to breathe, and most of her breaths were very awkward, jerking gasps. It is awful to see her breathing like that, really since she was born. Her oxygen levels dropped really low this morning, and she has continued to struggle. I found myself standing over her, constantly trying to breathe for her.

This evening she was placed back on the ventilator. While we are saddened by this need, when we got back to her room after she was re-intubated, we found some peace. Sofie has never looked so comfortable since she has been born. She is breathing easily and hopefully will be able to focus on rest and continued healing without the constant struggle for air. Luckily, my good friend and co-worker, Ted, was able to come to the hospital, and we were able to get some pictures of Sofie without the breathing tube.

We also found out that they have decided to do a repeat EEG tomorrow, but we are not exactly sure why. We missed the doctor, and he initially indicated no need to do another one. I am hoping this unplanned repeat of the EEG somehow becomes the miracle we have been waiting for. It is another chance to peek inside of Sofie's brain and hope that the prayers for a miraculous healing have been answered.

We believe the hopefully small setback of the ventilator allowed Sofie to rest and we; Mike, Sofie's night nurse, and I were able to witness Sofie move each of her hands. When we heard the nurse describe what we witnessed as "seemingly purposeful movements," our hearts filled with joy.

I know Mike and I are holding onto every possible bit of hope, so to hear the nurse say this as well was monumental. It was small movements when we were lotioning her soft skin, a wiggle of a wrist and a squeezing grasp of my finger on the other hand. I cherish those small movements and hope there are many more to come. I believe Sofie will have the most restful night she has had thus far. I pray this rest gives her an opportunity to feel the prayers that have been coming from all over, to heal her little body, lungs, and brain. We would appreciate prayers that she will receive the energy and the ability to rise up literally and figuratively, to awaken and restore so many people's faith to a whole new level.

Sofie deserves every chance to be a little girl full of love, joy, and hope so that one day her eyes will meet us with recognition, and be filled with pure wonderment and awe like any little girl's eyes should be.

CHAPTER 8

DAY SIX OF LIFE: HANGING ON TO HOPE...

I don't even know what day it is. I can't believe that a week ago I started the laboring process and that in just about thirty minutes from now one week ago, what I thought would be the happiest moment of my life quickly became the scariest. My baby girl entered the world and was whisked out of me into a world that has been so cold to her. It is a world in which she was quickly placed on a ventilator, stuffed into the transport box, where I only peeked at her for seconds before she was taken to another hospital that seemed millions of miles away. She was greeted there by an ice-cold cap on her injured brain and tubes and wires everywhere, and that cruel start for her has continued.

Today started as every other day has since we got here. I pray until I fall asleep at night that I will wake up on my couch with my giant pregnant belly and will be able to tell Mike about this awful dream I just had.

But when I wake, the stale air of the hospital guest room catapults me back into our hellish reality.

I can still feel Sofie moving inside of me sometimes. I hate that those inside movements that I remember so well are the last that I have felt or witnessed.

We trudge to morning rounds with the medical team, which Mike appropriately describes as feeling like a public flogging every day. We sit and listen to the grim words that the medical team shares: coma state, nonresponsive, flaccid…each word rips my heart wide open.

We witnessed Sofie continuing to move throughout the day, slight wrist/hand movements, one good arm movement, and one good leg movement. Is it purposeful? I don't know. I pray that it is.

The plan for the day is to do another EEG for a couple of hours. They will once again connect these hideous wires and leads to my precious baby girl's beautiful head…and we wait. The neurologist came by much too quickly today. He is a wonderfully kind man, but when I see him come closer, I burst into tears.

He solemnly reviews her EEG and decides to keep it on overnight. He says that upon further review, the last EEG displayed sudden bursts of activity followed by hours of low voltage. They are definitely *not* seizures, and that is good. While her EEG remains abnormal, he says that now there is more activity. He now sees bursts of activity followed by eight to ten seconds of low voltage. Mike and I understand that this is grim. We understand that her EEG is not normal, but a level of medication they gave her initially to prevent seizures is still elevated, and the fact that we see some movement and there is more activity has to mean something, right? We are hanging onto that very hope. We continue to pray tirelessly for healing.

Sofie has touched so many lives; we have received about a hundred cards for her already. We read her every one. There has to be a bigger plan for her.

We continue to read to her, sing to her, talk to her, plead with her to wake up, plead to God to wake her up.

The medical team needs to see what she can do. Right now science is winning in their heads. The devastation of the injury is winning, but faith *has* to overcome that and show everyone that God can move mountains. Sofie will be an amazing proclamation of God's love and ability to conquer all. I believe she is on her way already with these small signs.

CHAPTER 9

DAY SEVEN OF LIFE: THE OTHER SIDE OF THE COIN...

Today it is the support from so many that has given me the strength to simply get out of bed. People have been sharing their admiration of my strength and faith, but sadly, I have never felt weaker. I wake up in the morning, and it takes every ounce of everything in my body and soul to even walk into that NICU. A mother should want to rush to see her baby, not be terrified by what lies ahead.

Once I am there, I truly do cherish every moment with her. Every chance we have to take a temperature, change a diaper, do her mouth care, we are there.

This morning, another one of my ongoing fears came true. The bad part about working in the place where your daughter is clinging to life is that you know every step of the game before it happens. I have been on the other side of this exact experience time and time again for eight years. I just don't know how we ended up on this side of things.

I knew it was just a matter of time until we heard these words, and today they arrived: "We've done everything we can do," "Palliative care," and "Let nature take its course." The medical staff has been amazingly supportive of us and where we are. Mike politely told them that we are not there just yet and that we feel she needs more time. Her phenobarbital level is still elevated; we are seeing some small signs of something that we believe is improvement. We are not there yet, and may we never have to be. Please take no offense; to those who work in palliative care, your services are beyond meaningful, but these are things we are just not ready or willing to face at this time.

Mike and I know we are clinging, barely holding on to anything right now. We are aware that our grasp onto hope is slippery at best. But we still dream of taking our precious baby girl home as a miracle story and proving that she just needed more time. We can't give up on that or her.

Sofie continues her little movements today. I know they are not enough for the medical team, but they are enough for us right now. This evening for the first time, her nurse, Laurie, and the respiratory therapist were able to elicit a carinal reflex (like a deep cough). Sofie had never done that before. We're sure the doctors think we are crazy when we run to them with these little progresses, but right now that is all we have. We are told that while these are things she hasn't done before, they wish they had seen these done days earlier. My heart is heavy.

We have been moved to a private room where we can now once again hold Sofie. Mike cradled her for hours. He has been so amazing through all of this, with her…with me. He is much better at focusing on the here and now while I find myself continuously trying to relive the moment she was born and with all my might, desperately trying to rewrite the ending.

I get to participate in more skin-to-skin contact with Sof for hours. We spent the entire day holding her, loving her, and she was able to be visited by lots of family. I still don't know how we got here, and I know that I never will. I know that even if there ever could be an answer, there could never be an answer good enough to explain any of this.

We love her so much, and I hope she feels that. We continue to receive an outpouring of support. Mike and I know she already is such a miracle, that in her short seven days of life, she has reached people's hearts across the country and globally, at least in New Zealand, Australia, Argentina, and India that we know of. How many seven-day-olds have that magnitude of power?

May God's power continue to work miracles in her. I pray that this captive audience that is following Sofie's story of survival and hope can witness firsthand the extraordinary power of prayer in healing for this little love.

We continue to pray for her, hope for peace for her, and wait as we face many more difficult days ahead. We are trying to focus on the very miracle that she is here, focus on the fact that we have this time with her, and cherish every single moment.

I continue to believe in hope.

CHAPTER 10

DAY EIGHT OF LIFE: LORD, GIVE ME STRENGTH...

Today we had to face head on what we have been facing in our fears and in our heads since we heard the words *brain injury* at birth. I would never have thought that at eight days old we would be making our precious baby a DNR (do not resuscitate). We would never have envisioned her homecoming from the hospital to include hospice and palliative care. But alas, here we are.

We have had to pull strength from each other and from all who have continued to keep our family in your hearts, thoughts, and prayers.

While I still feel completely robbed by this situation, we decided that it could have been slightly worse. We are blessed that we have been given the time we have with Sofie. We understand that had the delivery been just a few hours later, we would not have even have had that.

Through our tears and heartache, we have decided to celebrate Sofia every moment possible. We had lots of cuddle time, we sang to her, and we read her more stories and of course more of the hundreds of cards she has received. We were even able to get her dressed in her own outfit today from home, topped off with a very stylish hair bow. Sofia is absolutely beautiful, and we are focusing on these incredibly precious moments...even though they are much too short.

There are still many moments of weakness and tears, and I know that those will last a very, very long time. I'm not going to lie and say I don't still hope with every fiber in my being that Sofie will receive a miracle and wake up. I will cling to that wholeheartedly.

While this is all happening much too fast and we are not making any quick decisions, we have decided that Sofie will come home.

She deserves to be in her home, a place full of love that has been prepared for her from the minute we found out about her. She deserves to be among her belongings, which were purchased just for her, and not in this cold hospital room.

While the details have not yet been figured out, Mike and I know we want her home with us, for however long that may be.

Sofie, I promise I will love you every day for the rest of my life; you will be in my heart and a part of my soul forever. But please, baby girl, please wake up.

CHAPTER 11

DAY NINE OF LIFE: CAN ANYONE SLOW DOWN TIME?

I feel like my hope for a miracle fades with the passing hours of each day. I get out of the shower in the morning and can't believe how empty my body feels. I wish it were still filled with a healthy, active Sofie.

Mike and I looked through her ultrasound photos today and shared them with Nurse Laurie. It was a special moment. Mike and I were able to feel like normal, doting parents.

She was so alive in those photos. I can't believe those kicks that I felt in my stomach are the last ones I will likely ever witness from my baby girl. When I wake up each morning, I just want to be sick, and when I go to bed at night and have to walk away from her, I feel the same way.

Mike and I have to begin making phone calls on Monday to begin the unthinkable. How does one prepare mentally, emotionally, physically to make plans for this?

So many people are praying all over the world for this amazing little girl. How can the voices and prayers of so many in unity not be heard or answered? What happened to, "Ask and it shall be given unto you"? This sweet, little, innocent girl deserves a chance to live her life! I am so angry that God isn't listening. Mike remains strong, reminding me that I shouldn't be angry with the One who still has the ability to heal her. But I can't help but feel like these prayers are falling on deaf ears.

But today is today, and she remains right in front of me, so we continue to hold her, read to her, and love her. We share her with more family and soak up every precious minute. But why does the clock seem to be on fast forward?

CHAPTER 12

DAY TEN OF LIFE: THE LUCKY ONE...

No changes today for Miss Sofie, except that occasionally it appears that her eyes are a little more open than before. We keep hoping they'll pop open with an immediate recognition for us, but so far they are just half open and then closed again. We are not sure what this means or if it means anything at all.

We were able to bathe her today, shampoo her pretty hair, and just love on her. She was visited by more family and had more photos taken as she spent her first Super Bowl in Daddy's arms.

Mike was able to get home for a little bit today and brought her more of her own clothes that so many bought for her out of love and excitement. She is in some very snazzy pajamas from her cousin at the moment. She looks much cozier than in the hospital-issued attire.

I have received several messages today that others have received from various people about Sofia, some we have never even met. It is truly touching how much this little eight-pound, two-ounce baby girl(she's been growing) has captured the hearts of so many. She truly has changed how people are living and more importantly, how they are loving right now.

When we first told people we were pregnant (which was days after we found out because we were so full of joy), so many people told me, "Having children changes your life forever." While I don't think any of them expected our worlds to be changed quite like this, they are right. I think Mike and I have such an appreciation, through our sadness, of how our lives have changed.

It's not about sleepless nights in the traditional having a newborn sense. It's not about a messy house, diaper changes, or fewer nights out with friends. Instead our lives have changed forever on a much more significant level.

Our hearts have been lit ablaze for Sofie. She has helped me to feel a love that is so much stronger than I could have ever imagined and certainly can't put into words. I believe this is the purest form of love. It is complete, true, and vulnerable, and it hurts like hell.

Having Sofie has changed our lives forever. And I would live in this pain all over again for the opportunity we have had to love this little girl.

Mike and I are so proud of her. How many other ten-day-olds have impacted as many as she? She is amazing. She is a miracle. She is my daughter.

So many people have commented on how lucky she is to have me as her mama, and while I appreciate the kind words, I am the lucky one to be able to say that she is my daughter. I am the lucky one to be able to learn from her love. I, dear Sofie, am the lucky one.

CHAPTER 13

DAY ELEVEN OF LIFE: ANGER AND FEAR...

T oday has been a long day filled with visitors and some really difficult conversations. My day starts as usual, with that all-too-familiar feeling of nausea. I tell Mike that I wonder when I will go a day without feeling like I want to throw up constantly. My hunch is it will be a long while.

Last night and today I have nicely slipped into the stage of grief known as anger. This is an anger I have never known before. Not an, "I'm so angry but will feel better in a few hours or days" kind of anger. No, this is an innate, primal anger that is so powerful that it scares me. It is a stomp my feet, scream and cry, visceral anger that makes my body shake. I am not proud of this. I am not an angry person, and I don't know how to handle these strong feelings.

We walk into the NICU to see Sofie first thing this morning to find the poor physical therapist working with her. (I say poor because she doesn't deserve my nasty look accompanied by my nastier tone.) I am pissed. This is our time with our daughter. "Get away from her!" I want to yell, but I do not. Instead I cry. She continues to talk to us about the massage techniques we were taught last week. She won't test us today but maybe tomorrow. I want to scream at her, "Don't F-ing tell me how to touch my baby girl!" I know that won't help. But I just want her, everyone, all of this to go away! Stop taking time away from us and our daughter when we have so little.

We have some long conversations with several members of her medical team, especially with palliative care. It is very helpful but so incredibly sad. The plans can be in place this week. I don't know that I am ready. Will I ever be?

Mike and I are so supported by their team, but somehow this still feels all too fast. I have never been so terrified in my entire life. What if she just needs a little more time? What if she just needs two more weeks and then she'll wake up?

I feel paralyzed by fear. The very thought of leaving the hospital feels like I will be stepping outside completely naked.

As Mike and I continue to discuss the ugly details, the anger returns. We are visited by one of the hospital chaplains who has become more of a friend than a co-worker in the years we have worked so closely together. She is strong in her faith, but I can also see the anger she has toward this injustice. She doesn't try to say the right thing; she just allows Mike and me to organize our thoughts out loud.

We discuss buying a family plot, what we want to put on her prayer cards…things that are nowhere close to the questions we should be asking, like, "Which curtain is best for her beautiful room? Two sets of crib sheets or three?" I ask them, "Does the back of her card have to be a prayer?" Mike looks up at me from his chair, as if to inquire what I mean, but there is a twist of concern in his eyes. I asked this because there is a quote that is very touching that I would like to use in place of a prayer. But instead of explaining that, what actually falls out of my mouth is, "Can we just put a big 'F You, God!' on the back?" (This is for all of those who have commented on how faithful I have remained.)

This is an ugly truth, but it's how I feel today. God will have to forgive me for this later, but right now I'm a bit miffed with Him, to put it lightly. Mike quickly looks down in awe, and out of sheer embarrassment that I have just said this in front of the chaplain, but I know they both understand.

The nighttime brings stillness. No more visitors, no more details to discuss…for now. We get to hold our baby and enjoy the night with her.

I hope that holding her will ease my anger, but it just brings more tears. I just want to hold her and keep her forever in the literal sense. I don't know how to let that go...how to let her go.

This godforsaken journey that we should have never found ourselves on continues.

CHAPTER 14

DAY TWELVE OF LIFE...

Sofie remains the same today. She continues to slightly lift those eyelids, but her eyes remain unreactive. Her pupils are fixed and dilated. God, I hate those words. Every time Sofie does these little stretching movements, which we are told are a spinal cord reflex, I desperately command her, "Big stretch...wake up, wake up, wake up," just in case this is the one stretch that wakes her from her brain-injured slumber.

But it doesn't. I imagine her saying back to me in the sweetest of voices, "I'm trying, Mama, but it's just too hard."

It is...too hard for a precious baby girl. It is OK, Sofie. You just rest if you need to. All of my pleading in your ear to please wake up is so desperate, and I want it so badly. But I understand if it is just too hard. You just rest, my beautiful girl.

Our priest comes in today to anoint Sofia. He was kind enough to rush in the day we were admitted to baptize her as well. We have known Father Kraker for about four years. He is in his seventies, but in all of his years of priesthood, he has remained surprisingly relevant. He just understands people. He has a wonderful temperament that is warm and gentle, and he has not lost his sense of humor or his genuine compassion in all of the years he has been ministering.

Mike's parents were married at his church, and since they were deceased when we married, it was an important connection for us to be married there as well. Within our first meeting with Father Kraker, we knew we had found our spiritual home.

We were taken aback by his soft yet larger-than-life personality. We had also heard a rumor around town that he is known as "the singing priest." The night before our wedding, I joked with him about this title and playfully wondered if there would be a song on our big day. There sure was.

Nearly our entire homily was a classic Broadway tune that sang of love. It was spectacular. I later learned that Father Kraker had the opportunity, in his younger years, to sing on Broadway, but he walked away from that to continue his dream and calling to the priesthood. Today I am thankful for that choice.

Father Kraker sits in our presence, supporting us gently. Mike updates him on our plans to go home with hospice care.

I hold Sofie, and we take some photos. I find myself physically unable to pray out loud with Father Kraker. He speaks kindly as he squeezes my shoulder and whispers, "Sofia will either be a miracle or a saint."

My heart knows it will be both, but I say firmly, "I want her to be the miracle." My heart knows that she already is.

Our meeting comes to a close, and what was a difficult yet peaceful interaction is quickly replaced by the rapid continuum of life in the NICU.

Those who know me know that I am not one for confrontation, yet it is surprising how easily it comes when you are the voice for your child. I had a little tiff with the new doctor caring for Sofie today; apparently some tears and making him feel badly were all it took for him to finally succumb to what we needed and understand a glimpse from a powerless parent's perspective. It felt good to be able to stand up for Sof and feel some sense of control in this helpless situation.

While being a family in the hospital where I work has been an equal combination of a curse and a blessing, today it was a blessing.

I feel so thankful to have an amazing amount of support and knowledge at my fingertips in the people I work closely with every day. Having them support Mike and me through our difficult journey as we face these unbearable decisions brings me some peace, though I remain terrified. I am thankful for their perspectives.

I tell some close friends today how it's so strange that I can see my parallel life at this very moment. I can actually play it in my head like a movie. We deliver our baby, they throw Sofie on my belly, she cries…she is fine. We rejoice as we announce her arrival to the world. We take the normal hospital photos, quickly share her pictures so everyone can see this stunning baby girl. Fast forward…we are home. I am holding her up in her beautifully decorated nursery and kissing her everywhere. I take pictures of her throughout the day and text them to Mike because he is back at work. We bathe her, read her stories in her nursery, and peek in on her sleeping soundly. It is just as we had hoped. I see us adoring this little girl in the normal, "We just had a baby" sense. This family seems so happy.

It is so strange how that world seems just out of reach, yet we can't get there. My heart gets heavy. I want to be them. We *were* them. I want to trade this crappy world for that one, so Sofie can know what the world should have been for her.

I mourn the entire lifetime that I had created for us with Sofie. It's like how a girl plans her wedding from the time she is a child. It was the same way when we got pregnant. In this year alone, we have so many plans that include Sofie. How do we face all of those things without her here? I want to throw up just thinking about it.

We share the day with more visitors. It was wonderful to share in their love and support. Sofie received an incredible gift today that I know I will treasure forever. It is the most beautiful musical snow globe with her name delicately inscribed, as delicate as her soft, velvety skin. It is gorgeous. Butterflies and tender silver flowers with just a touch of pink jewels are spiraled inside. The softest blue sparkles dance down toward the bottom while a lullaby plays. I know there will be many days when I will play this and remember my little girl.

Mike holds the snow globe close to Sofie's ears as it plays its melody for her. I hear him say, "Whenever we see a butterfly, we will think of you." He is so in love with his daughter.

Our plan to date—we will take Sofie home on Monday with hospice in tow, where she will be removed from her ventilator as we hold her in her nursery. We will surround her in absolute love.

God, if You are out there, if You can hear me, if You are listening at all, please consider that miracle…*now*!

CHAPTER 15

DAY THIRTEEN OF LIFE: DREAMING OF SOFIE...

I'm not sure if I already shared this, so if I did previously, forgive my confused, tired, and very sad brain.

Two nights ago I dreamed of Sofie for the first time since she has been born. I was lying down in the grass and holding her over my head, bringing her down to me to kiss her and raising her up again. Sofie was just giggling and giggling. There was an old, dear friend that I noticed when I lifted her over my head who was standing over us, quietly watching with a "this is exactly the way it should be" look on his face as he sang to my baby girl.

It was so comforting to hear those giggles. I know she will be giggling soon, with a perfectly healed brain, just giggling as a happy and healthy baby should.

I dreamed of Sofie again last night. This was a different dream. We were both patients in the hospital. We both required life support. Sofie was doing well. She was snuggled up against my face, cheek to cheek, and I could feel her warmth moving closer to me. They let me hold her hand as they were trying to intubate me. I remember feeling like I couldn't breathe. I couldn't call for the nurse; I simply had no breath.

That is how I feel. I am suffocating. I wish with every loss of breath I have, Sofie would get stronger. I recall a family I have worked with

53

in the past where the prognosis was poor for this mother's son. She exhaustingly would ask our staff to transplant her brain to him. She was serious.

Many times the staff, including me, would start to groan at her lack of understanding of this ridiculous statement. I now share that same desperation with her. I understand where that ridiculous comment comes from. It is in fact not ridiculous at all. It is so true; I would give anything to heal Sofie—my breath, my brain, my health, my life. For now I'll have to settle for giving her all of my love.

CHAPTER 16

DAY FOURTEEN OF LIFE: A TIP FOR THE NURSE...

Last night Mike and I had another snuggly night with Sof. We take turns holding her for hours, reading her what we believe are her favorite books, and just cuddling her while we watch some droning TV, pretending that this is somehow normal.

We put her in her PJs, tuck her in, dim the lights, turn on her soft, calming lullabies, and kiss her goodnight.

This morning I came in early and noticed that Sofie was in different pajamas and different blankets. We have been saving all of the ones she has been using, but the blankets that swaddled her soft skin last night are now gone, and she had all-new bedding. My heart was sad. Sofie has been refluxing some of her feeds due to her lack of a gag reflex. It has been in pretty good amounts, and it breaks my heart to watch her go through just one more thing. I assumed she had spit up during one of her overnight feedings and asked her morning nurse.

Apparently she did not spit up, which is good. Apparently one of her nurses just decided to change her pajamas and bedding, "just because she likes to."

I am angry. As her parent right now, in this situation, there is so little Mike and I get to have, get to control, and get to be a part of.

Tucking our little girl in at night, in the PJs we picked out, seemed like a little bit of normalcy. I am mad that she altered that.

Tip to nurses: please consider this when you are doing something "just because." It may be such a small, meaningless task to some, but to me, it was monumental. I likely only have four to five days left of selecting which one of her cozy, warm outfits will grace her body as she sleeps. Only a few hours are left where I can change my baby girl into her pajamas and kiss her goodnight. Please...don't mess with that.

Would I go into your nursery and change your baby's clothes in the middle of the night just because? Oh wait, we aren't in her nursery; we are in this crappy hospital room.

Today we had a long day of visitors, and it was wonderfully exhausting. There are no words to explain what it is like watching loved ones coming in to say good-bye to your new baby girl. It is just not right. My head still spins, still hopes this is a dream. I just want to keep her forever. I don't understand why I don't get to. I don't understand why she doesn't get to live the amazing life we had planned for her.

I want to watch her grow, see what she will look like, what she will be interested in—sports, music, art? I want to see her go to her first father-and-daughter dance with her daddy, teach her how to put on makeup, talk to her about boys, and see her get ready for prom and have a family of her own someday. I don't understand why she doesn't get to have those things or why we don't get to witness them.

We were able to do some memory making with Sofie today—handprints, footprints, prints in plaster, little fingerprints I can turn into necklaces for her little cousins, who have been eagerly awaiting her arrival. I glance around the room at the piles of prints we have made. Is this all I will have left of her when she is gone? My cell phone rings, but I don't recognize the number. I pick up my phone but hesitate. I decide not to answer. Perhaps this was a little divine intervention. I'll thank Him later for this.

I listen to the voicemail. It is the director of her daycare, confirming our need for a space in April. I sob.

Tomorrow we meet with hospice. That makes my stomach turn. My head knows this is the best decision for her little body, but my heart wants so much more. I know we are going to get home and I am going to scream, "I've changed my mind!" I wonder what they would do. I imagine myself walking out of the room before they take the tube out, feeling like if I walk away, maybe it just won't happen.

I will not walk away. I will sit with my baby girl, holding her every second until she is free—free from this life that has been so unfair to her. Though it will be the most painful experience of my life, I will be by her side.

As much as I hate everything about this hospital at this time—walking into the NICU to see my baby, having to wait for the nurse to help me with the tubes and wires so I can hold her at their convenience, being here at all—it is amazing how this suddenly feels like a comforting routine. At least Sofie is here.

What do I do once we are home and she is not? How do Mike and I go on forever changed by this little princess but having everything around us return to the way it was before we were blessed with her? I sadly find comfort in this hospital routine, and I am so scared to leave it behind.

I talk with Sofie's nurse tonight. She asks me if I realized that Monday is Valentine's Day. Mike and I had not when we were making our home-going plans. She asks kindly, "Do you want to change the day?"

I appreciate her sensitivity but confidently reply, "No, it seems perfect to take her home on that day. A day known for love *should* be the day that she enters her home for the first time."

And with an instant flash of recall to the day I learned I was having a girl, I know exactly what dress she will be wearing home: her Valentine's Day dress.

Tonight there is more cuddling to be done, more PJs to pick out, and more kisses to give. She will be the most beautiful Valentine for her daddy.

CHAPTER 17

DAY FIFTEEN OF LIFE:
A PEACEFUL NIGHT...

Last night when the last of the visitors left, we found ourselves alone with our baby girl. Tucked away in our little cave, which I mean endearingly, it is such a blessing to draw the curtain, close ourselves in, and be a family—just the three of us, the way it was intended.

While we may not be in the comfort of our own home or using the beautifully put together nursery for Sof, when that curtain is drawn, this is our haven. We continue to hold, stare at, memorize, and love our little girl.

One piece that has gone unmentioned by me in my wide range of emotions but has certainly not been unnoticed is how amazing my husband has been. Over two weeks ago he had never even changed a diaper and wasn't really thrilled about the idea of doing so.

In the last fifteen days, I have watched him not only rise through this devastation but do what I so often could not—just focus on the very moment we are in and enjoying that moment with his little girl. He has said, "This is the only parenting we know right now." He is right. I have remained so focused on my pain, my hurt, my lost dreams, my feeling robbed that I feel like I have missed out on so many opportunities to just be in the very moment, soaking up my little girl. I am trying to be better at that.

Mike is an amazing daddy. I watch him eat her toes and fingers, kiss her endlessly, and change her diaper like a pro while carefully protecting her breathing tube. He has learned more about ventilators, pulse ox machines, EEGs, and NG feedings than he should ever have had to, but he takes it all in stride because he loves his daughter. That piece is beautiful, even in the middle of this pain. That part I will be sure to treasure.

Daddy headed to bed a bit earlier last night because he had some very unpleasant tasks to take care of this morning. It is amazing how meeting with a funeral home to make prearrangements for a day you hope will never come can leave you drained and exhausted. But I was able to steal some time alone with Sofie.

I held her for hours, and we talked. Well, I talked; I hope she listened. I tell her about all of her loved ones who have gone before her who I know will care for her when she gets to heaven. I speak of her cousin Jamie, just eleven years old, who I know will be waiting to babysit her until Mama or Daddy can be there. I know she will keep her occupied with games and the kind of love a little baby girl deserves.

I tell her of her grandparents and assure her not to worry, that she will know exactly which one is her grandpa because he looks just like her daddy. I picture him rocking her and cradling her in his lap… protecting her. I tell her that one day, I hope she is the first one to greet me. I see Jamie bringing her to me, placing her gently in my arms, and giving me back all of the moments I yearn for now, and Sofie is well, restored to health.

I tell her not to be scared—that even though Mama is upset with God right now, He will take good care of her. He *better* take as good of care of her as I was going to. That is the least He can do.

I tell her how much I love her, the tiniest of things I will miss about her, and how I will love her forever and make her a part of my every day. I talked to Sofie so much when she was growing inside, and I find myself still talking to her when I am away from her room. I know that will continue.

I tell her that I don't want to let her go from this physical world, but I understand that is what she needs. I will always make sure she is celebrated. I yearn for the day when someone who doesn't know our current situation but recognizes that I have had my baby wishes me a joyful, "Congratulations!" that I can just smile and say, "Thank you," as I revel in my pride for being her mom while not being bogged down by such sadness. I am getting there.

I tell her that my tears are not a sign of being disappointed in this hand that we were dealt but are out of pure love for her as she has become my entire heart.

I live for the day when I am going about my daily routine and someone asks me if I am related to the Sofia Dente who has inspired the world. I will look at them proudly, proclaiming that I am her mom.

I talk and talk and realize that it is 2:45 a.m. It was a beautiful night.

I put her in her pajamas, tuck her in, read her our favorite goodnight story, dim her lights, put on the music, kiss her a hundred times, and slowly walk away.

For the first time since we have found ourselves here, I do not cry myself to sleep. I love you, Sofia Isabella. I am so proud and honored to be your mother.

CHAPTER 18

DAY SIXTEEN OF LIFE:
A THANK YOU TO A NURSE...

This morning I walk back into the NICU after our special night, to find a familiar nurse caring for her at the bedside. I notice that Sof is in the pajamas I put her in before I left, and her room is unchanged from the way I left it.

I notice that not only have things been unchanged, but the nurse has continued to restart her lullaby cd so she can continue to hear the soft music. She does her assessment in the dimmed lights to not disturb the sleeping Sofie.

It is a noticeable difference from twenty-four hours ago. This nurse has not only cared for her the way I would hope and want, but she also took the time to do the little things, that as her mom, mean the world to me.

She preserved the environment I had created for Sof before I went to bed. She provided the loving touches that show she is not only doing her job but is truly caring for my baby girl.

I thank her for that. She feels that is a small thing; I tell her it is not. It meant the world to walk into that this morning.

"When I see your face, there's not a thing that I would change, because you're amazing, just the way you are." Welcome, Sofia Isabella!

This was the way I had planned to announce Sofie's arrival to our world. I'm sorry it took me until now to be able to joyfully announce the arrival our baby girl deserves.

—FACEBOOK STATUS UPDATE: FEBRUARY 12, 2011

CHAPTER 19

DAY SEVENTEEN OF LIFE...

Sofie enjoyed the last day of visitors today, and it was lovely—a day of celebration for her. We have asked for no more visits to allow Mike and me to selfishly steal every last moment with Sofie, tonight and tomorrow, before our homecoming on Monday.

With each hour, with each item from her room that I pack away, I become more and more frightened. When we chose Monday to be our home-going day, it seemed so far away. How did it arrive so quickly?

I'm not sure I'm ready; I'm not sure I'll ever be. Mike said to me today that six years from now would still seem too soon, and he is right. I still just want to keep Sofie forever. I want to rock her, hold her, read to her, sing to her, kiss her a million times each day. I fear the void I will feel next week.

I still weep for what we should have had with her. I am so proud that she has touched the world, but we really would have been more than content with complete anonymity. We would have rather had everything be just the way it should have been, the three of us holed up in our house, enjoying every typical newborn moment.

But we can't have that, though I don't understand why, and I never will.

I promise Sofie that I will continue to visit her and read her our bedtime story often. I tell her not to be scared. God, I don't want her to be scared. I don't want her to know that I am terrified.

This will be my last update until we bring our little love home.

I will continue to update Sofie's incredibly large "family," but I want to soak up every last second with her these next few days.

May the next update I write be a miraculous one, one where I can announce that faith has won over science and we can share in the joyous healing of this sweet inspiration.

Mike and I know what is ahead, but we are still hanging on to every shred of hope right up until that last possible second, that last breath. We imagine them taking out the breathing tube and having her gag, cough, and cry, much to everyone's surprise.

We dream of us drifting to sleep with her in our arms as she continues throughout her first night at home and we are joyously awakened to the sound of her crying.

We understand that is not likely how Monday will go. We understand that we will hold her as they remove the breathing tube, and we will likely watch our baby girl slip away from life with us as we cradle her in our arms, each breath a little bit less life-giving than the last. But we have to hold on to something.

Until then, we have tonight and tomorrow. We have more stories to share and more love to give. I still need to tell her all about boys before she gets up there so she understands that the ones who tug at her angel wings are the ones who like her the most.

CHAPTER 20

THE JOURNEY HOME: A LENGTHY TALE OF OUR LAST TWO DAYS...

O ur last day at the hospital was filled with so much emotion. As much as we have hated being here, we really take comfort in this new familiar setting. It makes me smile to hold my daughter and be able to look down at her amazingly formed, heart-shaped lips and know exactly at what times of the day she is "pocketing" her milk and needs to be suctioned; I am right every time I tell the nurse.

It makes Mike and me smile when we notice her heart rate increase and her peaches 'n' cream complexion get slightly flushed as we can tell that she will need a diaper change. We are right every time. I love that I can tell exactly how she will turn her little head when I kiss the top of it and stroke her wonderfully silky hair.

Weeks ago I wondered how we would know which one of Sofie's cries meant what. Is she hungry? Tired? Overstimulated? I read all the books and was convinced I wouldn't be able to tell what she would need. I find comfort in knowing these things about her now. While certainly not in the traditional parenting sense, we do know Sofie, we are able to pick up on her little tricks, and knowing we have understood them is so comforting.

Our last full day at the hospital brought some unexpected stress to our planned day of snuggling. Sofie had a new nurse over the weekend for two days. She took loving care of Sofie, which is all we ask.

I believe she was trying to offer comfort and complimentary thoughts on Saturday when as I was holding my baby girl she said, "You and Mike are so brave to take her home on Monday and remove her from the ventilator. I couldn't do it." She leaned down close to Sofie and continued, "I would just have to hold you, love you, read to you, and sing to you forever."

I thought to myself, *I can do that too! I want those things too!* I began to doubt myself and our decision. I want those things, selfishly, but that is not fair to my precious girl.

I stayed up with Sofie extra late Saturday night, reading to her and enjoying one of our late-night chats that I will cherish forever. I tell her to please give me signs throughout my life so I know she is OK. I ask her to visit me in my dreams so I can take comfort in knowing she is all right and can receive solace in seeing her again. I ask her to please look over her mama because these next few days, weeks, months, years, and many days throughout my life are going to be so hard as I will yearn for her touch and miss her entirely.

I ask her to please watch over Daddy and check on him now and again too because I know how much he loves his little girl, and he is always so strong around Mama, but I know he'll need reassurance that she is OK as well.

I leave her bedside after a million kisses, to which I imagine her saying, "Oh, Mom!" with a teenager kind of attitude but knowing that secretly she is glad to have been kissed. I walk away and feel somewhat at peace.

Mike arrives to her bedside before me on Sunday morning. I walk in to find him and that same nurse standing intently over Sofie's crib.

"She has a gag reflex," Mike offers flatly.

The nurse is squealing with such joy, "She has a gag reflex!"

I have wanted to hear these words for three weeks, but today hearing them makes me feel like I have just been kicked in the stomach. She is gagging? What does that mean for her? Is she starting to wake up more? We are taking her home in twenty-four hours to take her off of life support. If she is going to start doing new things, she needs to do it now! Does she just need more time?

68

The nurse proudly demonstrates this gag reflex over and over for us to see, saying she didn't tell any staff but wanted us to see it. I think, *If she is gagging and doing something new, shout it from the rooftop!*

She says to me that she is so surprised given my intuition through-out my pregnancy that I am not second guessing our decision more. My heart drowns in sorrow.

I have been second guessing our decision to bring her home every second of every day. She looks closely at Sofie and says to her, "I could just never let you go. I would just have to keep you alive to stare at that pretty little face every day."

I want that too! I want to stare at that gorgeous face every second of every day! Does she think that I want to bury my daughter? But if she is gagging now, maybe she will wake up. Maybe I can keep her.

We speak to several helpful staff members on Sunday evening who know us and our little girl. Her night nurse, who has cared for her several times, is aware of the day's findings. She does not feel that Sofie is gagging or gagging well if she is at all, and while she does move slightly with the stimulation, it isn't groundbreaking or new. She has been doing that.

We decide to have another full neurology exam in the morning, a head-to-toe assessment, to determine if there are any new changes or signs of progress. We are not sure what this means for our Monday, but after speaking with more staff, we recognize that even if she is truly gagging, that does not give her a quality of life. Is it fair to keep her alive because she can posture (abnormal movements), do minimal purposeful movements, which are far and few between, and gag? It has been twenty days; we know her brain cannot recover. But if she is gaining more function, does she just need more time?

Monday morning comes with such fear. Her full neurology assess-ment does show an occasional weak gag, but it is only triggered incred-ibly deep in her throat, not where it should be to protect her airway. The rest of her exam, which we watched solemnly, remains unchanged. We watch the doctor painfully stimulate our baby with no reaction. She pokes at her eyes, roughly pinches her skin to elicit any reaction... nothing.

The outcome: the same devastating news that we have heard too many times. Yet this time, we were prepared for that. We find some reassurance with those results as we feel back at peace with our decision to free Sofie from these struggles, these harsh machines and exams, and let her find peace.

We take a lot of photos, and we prepare for our journey home. It is time. We dress Sofie in that navy blue dress with the red argyle hearts, which was bought for her so long ago and intended for such a different purpose. She is breathtaking and accessorized tastefully with a white hair bow and some white tights to keep her tiny legs warm. She swims in the tights. As heavy as our hearts are in this very moment, we can't help but giggle at how silly these baggy tights look on her slim legs.

The transport team shows up. They will let me ride in the back with Sof as long as I sign a waiver. I am glad to. Mike will follow behind the ambulance.

They also make special arrangements not to have Sofie ride in the transport box that whisked her away from the birth hospital. She is permitted to ride on a stretcher with me by her side. I know this is not their protocol, and I am so grateful.

Watching this tiny, delicate girl on the giant stretcher is heart wrenching. I follow slowly, terrified. A rush of cold wind greets me as I enter the back of the transport ambulance, and I barely notice that this is the first time I have felt outside air in three weeks.

Sofie and her equipment are loaded into the back right next to me. I am terrified as we had to discuss the possibility of her dying in the ambulance. If something should change unexpectedly, they will call Mike and pull over to have him join us if that happens. God, please don't let that happen.

The ride to our house seems to take forever and come too quickly all at the same time. We turn on our street, and I see our house. It looks so different.

I am allowed to carry Sofie inside while the respiratory therapist breathes for her with every pump of her hand.

I walk into our living room and barely recognize it. This doesn't feel like my house. I don't even know where I am.

We sit on our couch with Sofie on our lap as our good friend Ted sets up for some family photos that we will treasure forever.

Our home slowly becomes familiar; I know it is because Sofie is here.

We take our photos, walk Sofie around her house, place her in some of her things—her swing, her bouncer, her crib. She should get to feel these things.

We slowly walk her up to the nursery; I know what this means. We change her diaper on her changing table using her soft, pink, fuzzy changing pad. We sit with her in her glider. They give us time. We talk to her; I cry. We tell her how much we love her and that she is loved by so many.

I read her our bedtime story while Mike cradles her. Then we tell the team that we are ready—ready for Sofie to be free from these machines, from these struggles, from her fight.

They remove the breathing tube as Mike holds her while I am sitting right next to them, practically lying in Mike's lap to be as close as possible. Sofie immediately turns dusky shades that you never want to see a baby turn, and she is silent. I see Mike catch the doctor's eye and whisper, "I think she is gone." It has been minutes. I sob, "I thought we would have more time."

We do. After a few minutes of what seems like nothing, Sofie regains her color. She begins breathing on her own, though ineffectively. They give her medicines to ensure she is comfortable. She has some noisy breathing, but at the same time, she looks peaceful. She does not appear to be struggling. We are told that she is exhibiting signs that she is actively dying. We hold her, switching her between the two of us, for hours.

The medical staff leaves. Only one hospice nurse and a palliative care doctor remain with us. They stay on our first floor, respecting our privacy in Sof's nursery.

We read to her. We put on her lullabies; we dim her lights and light up her room with an adorable stuffed turtle that fills the room with a soft glow of blue stars. We continue to hold her and love her.

As the hours pass, Sofie continues. We continue to give her medicine to ensure her comfort. She is so strong.

Mike and I take turns speaking to her. "You can let go, baby girl. You can go to sleep."

"Mama and Daddy are so proud of you, so proud to be your parents."

"It's OK, little one. You can go to sleep. Rest, sweet baby girl, just rest."

Still she fights. As the night comes to a close, around midnight, hospice and palliative care check in with us, and together we decide to have them leave. We believe Sofie wants it to be the three of us before she will allow herself to go. They teach me how to give her meds and how to suction her if needed, and they leave.

We get into comfy clothes, Sofie included, and lay her on the floor in her pillow between Mike and me. We all have soft, fuzzy blankets, and Mike and I snuggle as close to Sofie as we can get. Occasionally we drift to sleep for seconds; occasionally I pick her up and cradle her in my arms. I am fighting my exhaustion, but I don't want to miss a minute that we have with her.

At 3:00 a.m., I give her more medication. Mike is sleeping next to her. I pick her up unassisted, hold her, and kiss her. I tell her that it's OK, that she can go. I lay her back in her pillow at 4:00 a.m. I am so tired. I set my alarm for 4:30 a.m. in case I doze off. I turn over, holding her tiny, cool hand, and drift to sleep.

I have a very fast-paced stress dream. Sofie's godmother and I are in a big city. It is chaotic; we can't find what we are looking for. We are running in and out of coffee shops searching for something. Then suddenly, overpowering the dream, as if the audio doesn't match the video, I can clearly hear a child giggling. The visual in my dream never changes—busy streets of a big city—but I can clearly hear giggling echoing overhead. The me in the dream doesn't seem to notice the giggling, but the slumbering me sure does. The giggles are so loud in comparison to the rest of the dream, in a perfect echo effect.

The giggles abruptly stop when I am startled and awakened by Mike. It is 4:16 a.m. He tells me that he isn't sure Sofie is breathing anymore. We stare at her intently as we stroke her cool face and hold her ice-cold hand. She releases two very small breaths, turns her head a touch, and looks at peace. It is 4:20 a.m. He says we should call hospice. I ask to wait just a little longer. We lay with her, crying, saddened, relieved that she is at peace. She looks so beautiful, so angelic, so at rest. After ten minutes, I call hospice. I sob when I ask for the on-call nurse and have to give the patient's name.

The doctor is on her way to "pronounce" my baby girl. I am cradling her in my arms while we wait. She arrives and lovingly checks our daughter. She tenderly whispers, "Well, Miss Sofie, it appears that you have done what you needed to do." I think, *That is so much more caring than hearing, "Time of death, 5:01."* We are so thankful for her kindness.

I prepare a bath for Sofie, bathe her in her own whale-shaped tub, using her own very girly washcloths, her own soaps, and her fuzzy, pink, hooded towel. We dress her again in her cozy pajamas, make some final handprints, and wait. The funeral home has been called, and they are on their way.

They show up, and I don't want to hand her over. I know she is gone, but I still want to keep her.

I sit, cradling her in my arms, while Mike and the funeral home folks speak. They are very kind and patient; I know they will regard her with the love and respect she deserves.

I finally feel able to place her in her car seat—well, not really, but I know their patience is only going to last for so long. Mike carries the car seat to the car, and we strap her in. I shudder as I hear the door slam closed in the loudest and cruelest way. We stand in the cold and watch her about to be driven away in an unfamiliar car with an unfamiliar person. I am soaked in my own tears.

I watch from the window as they pull out of our driveway. I can see her tiny, cold, slumped head in the car seat as they slowly back away and turn out of view. With every inch further the car gets, my heart breaks more and more.

The house feels so empty. I'm not sure what to do from here. I'm not sure how to do anything. I want them to bring her back.

The rest of the day is not easy; I know there will be many more that won't be. I am angry, I cry, and I just want Sofie!

I know it will take a long, long time before I feel even a little bit right about any of this. I may never feel that way.

I look around our house at all of the hand and footprints of her. Is this all I have left? I tell Mike that all I have is sore breasts and one small stretch mark to show for all of this. I know that isn't true. He tells me that we have so much more. I know we do, but I am so angry, sad, and scared.

I don't know how to handle this; I don't know how to feel normal. For right now, I hang on to last night. The three of us, snuggled in her nursery, closely together, not bound by any machines, tubes, or wires, with her lullabies on and her room aglow with blue stars. It was a peaceful ending to a really awful situation.

I love you, Sofie, more than I could ever have imagined my heart loving anything or anyone. I know you needed to go, sweet baby girl. I will miss you and love you forever and will look forward to reminders of you until I am able to hold you and rock you in my arms once again. Be at peace, sweet angel. Be at peace.

Last night was the first night I've spent away from Sofie in ten months. I hated it. I miss you, baby girl.

—F<small>ACEBOOK STATUS UPDATE</small>: F<small>EBRUARY</small> 16, 2011

CHAPTER 21

A NEW WORLD...

oday was the first day that everything was different—truly different. Yesterday morning we had Sofie for a little while, even after she had passed. We bathed her, held her, and dressed her. Today I had no Sofie. I find myself developing some new habits, one being pacing. I literally pace around the house from the moment I wake until I finally muster up the ability to take a shower for the first time since Monday. I try to start something—laundry, cleaning, going through the mail, organizing some of the hundreds of items that lay around our house from the hospital...anything...but I cannot. I simply pace.

I watch Mike jump into tasks. He is busy submitting her obituary, creating an online guest book, uploading photos, going for a run. He is amazing. I know he is so hurt inside, but his strength is focused on celebrating Sofie's life, living in the love she taught so many. I, on the other hand, am broken. I pace and pace, and occasionally I sit and cry... well, sob really. I clutch the blanket that she was covered in when she died. I clutch everything that touched her, and I sob.

I want so badly to feel connected to her again the way we were for ten months. I beg Sofie and God to send me a sign that she is OK. I just need to know she is OK.

When we were in the hospital, Mike told Sofie that every time we see a butterfly, we will think of her. One night during my late-night chats with Sof, I told her of another reminder of her. Butterflies and one other thing; I reserve that other sign for just Mike, Sofie, and me. It is our little secret. I cry and cry on the floor, begging for any sign that she is OK.

I eventually muster up some strength about half an hour later and continue to pace. I convince myself to take a shower. We have to go to the funeral home today.

As I head upstairs, I notice something nearby. It is the secret sign I told Sofie about. Is it just a coincidence? Why do I doubt it? When did I become so cynical? It must mean something! I find some comfort in this secret sign. I am grateful. I hope this means that she is all right. I know I'll need many more signs to feel more comfort, but this is a start.

Mike and I leave early for the funeral home; we have to pick up new tights for my baby girl. The tights she wore home did not fit well when we put them on her petite legs. They are not good enough for her, and she deserves perfect tights.

Against my better sense, I suggest Babies R Us. It's the very one I spent just about every weekend in preparing for Sof's arrival. In the store, I try so hard not to cry as I look over all the new Easter dresses and beautiful spring outfits. We should be shopping with Sof, buying a ridiculous amount of clothes and accessories to adorn her in for her first holiday. How is she not here? I feel my eyes well with tears. We find the tights and head to the checkout aisle.

Mike walks quickly ahead. I feel myself slowing down. I begin to take in the things I see around me. I eye an aisle filled with bottles of Dreft baby detergent. We have two at home. I have a moment where I literally want to throw myself down on the ground, kicking, punching, and screaming. I refrain...barely.

We get to the checkout aisle. The girl behind the counter politely asks, "How are you today?"

Mike responds with an upbeat, "Not too bad." I am angry at his answer. I look down, staring intently at the ground.

This is a new talent I have discovered since our admission to the hospital. If I don't make eye contact with anyone, maybe these things aren't really happening. In the delivery room when we got our awful news, I covered my eyes with my hands and wouldn't look at anyone. When we got to the NICU and received more bad news, again the hands assumed their position covering my eyes, and I looked down. When people would come to visit us who I didn't have the strength to see, I would stare at the ground until they left. I fully realize this is the same thought process as a four-year-old, but I truly believe that if I had looked up during any of those moments, I simply wouldn't have survived.

So once again in Babies R Us, I stare at the ground. I'm sure this checkout girl thinks I am rude. She's probably thinking, *Why is such a nice guy with such a bitch? Poor guy, he can do better than her.* But I don't care. I can't even fake it right now.

Doesn't she know I am buying these tights for my dead daughter? Doesn't she know we are on our way to the funeral home right now instead of celebrating that my baby girl is three weeks old today? No, she doesn't know. No one in this outside world knows.

This outside world doesn't feel safe in my new broken state. I know the world continues despite our tragedy, but I just didn't expect it to hurt so badly. The world's ignorance to my pain is piercing.

Before the funeral home, Mike stops at a car wash. We go through. I remember how I used to be terrified of these when I was little. Today it feels symbolic.

We enter, the cleansing begins, and it gets darker as we proceed. You can barely see ahead but move forward because the track gently pushes you along. The brushes hit hard; they are so loud. The car gets so dark. We continue, being nudged gently. The outside light starts to shine in, but the windows are so blurred from the soap. Slowly the car gets washed clean, and I can once again see the outside light in full. I hope I am being gently nudged by my baby girl to be slowly pushed from this dark place into the light once again. I know that's a tall order for a twenty-one-day-old angel, but she has done so much already. I know she can and will do this.

We continue to the funeral home and discuss our daughter's memorial. May no other parents ever have to face such a task.

I tell Mike how I just don't know how to "be" in this new world. I feel so disconnected from everything I knew. It's odd to me as we sit at the funeral home making plans that Mike is the jovial optimist, sharing how he just focused on enjoying Sofie for the time we had, and he did. He is an amazing father. And there I am, the one who was always the optimist in my previous life, always smiling, laughing, joking with my friends. I sit silently in this funeral home, completely broken. I don't know how to talk to people, how to interact with this world. I feel like I am in a parallel universe. I can almost convince myself this didn't happen, that my baby girl just hasn't arrived yet. It crushes me when I am sent back to the reality that she has come and is in fact already gone.

I do have some tender moments throughout the day. I look through our photos, and I share them with friends and family and smile. I think back to the special little moments we shared in the last three weeks, and I feel comforted. I know there will be days when these moments will come more frequently and the painful, heart-wrenching moments will come less and less. Until then, I need time.

I need to figure out who I am now. Our worlds have completely changed in the matter of just one hour—well, really with just one push. The world we had created and expected was suddenly traded for a world that is completely unfamiliar. I need to learn how to function in this new world, but for now, I just need to learn how to breathe in it.

Chapter 22

Day Two of a New Life...

I
t's weird how grief sneaks up on you. This morning when I wake up, I think, *I actually feel OK. I mean, I am heartbroken beyond belief, but I feel OK.* Apparently, as quickly as that moment of peace arrives, it is also taken from me.

Mike goes for a run, but when he starts to leave, he discovers a notice left on our door. Another delivery tag that reads, "Please call when you are home." He brings it to me.

Everyone's kindness is so thoughtful, but I do wish these were "Congratulations on your healthy new baby girl!" gifts. I call the flower company to let them know we are home. I want to tell them to just keep whatever they have. But they say they'll be out in an hour.

I attempt to go shower, and I lose it—and I mean lose it. I sit on our stairs, screaming, rocking, and crying as loud as can be. "I'm so sorry, Sofie!" I never wanted her to suffer a single day in her life, let alone for her entire life! I am crushed. I miss her. I want her back. I don't understand why I didn't get to keep her. I trudge to the shower and become hysterical. In the shower, it's hard to tell what is shower water and what are tears. Suddenly there is a loud knock at the bathroom door. Mike asks if I am OK. No, I'm not ok! But I lie and say yes.

I realize I may need to control myself better for the sake of those around me. I choke back my tears and dry off my deflated frame when I hear a knock at the outside door.

I am greeted by a delivery guy, and I pleasantly accept his gift. "Another f-ing fruit basket!" I want to shout. "Keep all of your damn fruit baskets! Just give me my baby back!" I feel so out of control.

I get dressed, and we head to the florist shop. We have to choose the arrangements for Sofie's calling hours and funeral. I walk in, and the owner kindly says, "I'm not even going to ask you how you are." She already knew why we were coming in. I thank God for her comment because I hate that question.

We pick out a wondrous display of light pink flowers for our beloved girl, and I do OK…well, better than I expected. We head back to the funeral home to finalize details.

The funeral home contact with whom we have been working proudly shows us her prayer cards, and I cry. He surprisingly questions my reaction, asking, "Do they look OK?"

I want to scream, "No they don't look OK! They have my daughter's name on them!"

Stupid question. Stupid guy. No, that isn't fair; he has been very kind to us. I am just so broken.

We are able to spend time with our baby girl today. They bring her to us, allow us to hold her newly prepared body. She looks different, and she feels different. She is heavy, and her skin is tight. Her lips have been sewn closed. She is beautiful still, but she does not look or feel like her.

I am grateful for this unorthodox time to hold her and kiss her. But she feels so different. Somehow, I find peace in this. I know she is gone. I know this isn't her. I would much rather recall my time holding her even after she had died because she still looked and felt like herself. Those are moments I will treasure.

We walk away from the funeral home with her empty car seat swinging in Mike's hand. It is all just so wrong.

We get home. We work on some special details for the services. We pick photos and arrange a slideshow. It feels healing.

The evening brings on a whole new task; I have to go buy dresses for her services.

I've been out of my house, my safe zone, too long today. This feels so surreal. Whose world am I living in? This certainly cannot be mine.

I quickly find a perfect dress for Sofie's funeral. It has to be perfect; it's for her.

For the calling hours, Sofie will be wearing that navy blue sweater dress with the red argyle hearts. That dress has become so meaningful to us, so it only seems right to have that be her final outfit. Mike bought a dark blue suit to coordinate with a blue and red tie.

I set out on a mission to find a dark blue dress. Apparently the recent tragedy in my life isn't enough; apparently this universe thinks it will be even funnier to add the impossibility of finding a dark blue dress into the mix. There is nothing that is even remotely close to being perfect enough for my baby girl.

I scour places—Dress Barn, Macy's, Dillard's, JC Penney, and every store in the mall in between. Nothing.

I find a suit jacket and skirt set in Dillard's that is OK. The color is right. If I can't find anything else, this could work. The woman brings me to the dressing room and says, "If there is anything else you need at all, just let me know."

I want to reply, "I need you to bring my daughter back," but I just nod as I choke back my tears.

I stare at myself in the mirror. Even in a crisp, new suit I feel so... disheveled. I feel so not myself. Never before have I ever worn a suit jacket like this. Then even more horror begins to set in when I realize... it has shoulder pads. I cry uncontrollably.

Shoulder pads are bad enough, but the thought of wearing them for the first time since 1990 to my daughter's calling hours is devastating. I already don't feel like the person I was four weeks ago, and this is not acceptable.

After I somewhat compose myself, I bring the suit back to the saleswoman. She asks if I need it in a petite instead. I want to scream, "No, I don't need a petite; I need my daughter not to be dead!" Instead I silently shake my head no.

I realize these thoughts of pure anger and heartbreak have been written about before. I know they probably become a tiresome routine to read about, but this is the world of the heartbreaking redundancy that has become my life.

I head to the shoe section, where a nice young man asks me what the shoes are for. I tell him for my dress and point it out. He clarifies, "No, I mean what type of event are they for?" I look at him through my exhausted, tear-stained eyes and simply reply, "Trust me, you really don't want to know," trying to spare him from the sadness and the story that will follow. He accepts that and helps me find beautiful shoes for Sof's funeral.

I think, *Maybe this is progress.*

CHAPTER 23

A HARD DAY AND SOME MOMENTS OF HEALING...

I always hear about how grief-stricken people have countless sleepless nights, and I wonder what I am doing wrong because for some reason, I am able to sleep just fine. And that makes me feel badly.

Waking up, however—that is another story. Every morning when I wake, it is a constant abrupt reminder that this isn't a bad dream, that this is all really happening and I have to face it all over again. I hate mornings.

Today it is beautifully sunny; the house is cool. Mike has opened all the windows. Somehow this spring-like air breaks my heart. I should be enjoying it with Sof today.

But Mike and I are preparing to go to the church to plan her funeral service. I set myself up to be angry at Father Kraker. I mean, why not? He works for God.

When we walk in, he greets me with the warmest hug, and I can't be angry. I want to melt into him. He feels safe. He has Sofie's obituary lying carefully in front of him.

We discuss our plans. I tell him of Sofie's impact on so many. I tell him that she loved music when she was inside of me and often was awakened into activity during mass when he would sing during his homily. He appears to soak up every word of Sofie like a young child hearing a wondrous tale for the first time. It touches me.

During some tearful moments, his dog, Minnie, runs into the room. I find such comfort in her. She looks at Mike and me with her innocent eyes and just wants to play and give loving attention. Maybe it's because she doesn't know, or maybe it's because she does. Either way, she shows no judgment, no discomfort, no awkwardness or sadness... just love.

We leave the church, and I ask Mike if we can try a few more places to resume my search for the perfect dark blue dress for calling hours. I had eventually settled on one last night, but I still hate it when I stand in front of the mirror, unable to recognize myself in its drapery pattern.

Without hesitation, Mike agrees, and we are off. We strike out at the Dress Barn, TJ Maxx; nothing, back to the mall. Macy's; again nothing. They do have a nice gray dress that is good enough for Sofie, but then I won't match her and Mike.

We once again try every store in between and again find nothing. We are walking through an unusually crowded mall for 10:30 on a Friday morning, and I start to cry. I cry out loud, "I just want a blue dress to match Sofie. Is that too much to ask?!" I cry harder.

Mike says in a determined voice, "Let's try Dillard's again." He knows how important this is to me in this moment. He will not give up until we find one. I love him for this.

We go back to Dillard's, and he immediately finds a dress that is navy blue—something I would consider "a Lori dress." It has small white polka dots on it, and it is pretty. I tell him no; it's too happy of a dress for this event.

He speaks in a commanding tone. "It's a perfect dress. You shouldn't be looking for a depressing outfit. This is perfect for celebrating Sofie's life." He is right...again.

I try it on, and it fits. We even find navy blue shoes to match. I have never worn blue shoes in my entire life; they look funny against my skin. Mike thinks they are perfect, so they must be. Perfect for Sofie.

We leave the store, and I feel better. I feel calm. We decide to grab something to eat, which I haven't really done since Tuesday other than a bite of a cracker, half an apple, and a handful of Junior Mints.

We sit down after we pick up a paper and review our little girl's obituary. We eat and talk. This moment feels almost normal. We talk about Sofie, and it feels good.

I look up and notice a familiar face from the not-too-distant past in line right near where we are eating. She knew I was pregnant but is not someone in a close circle. She probably doesn't know what has happened. I knew this moment was bound to come, someone leaping over to us eagerly awaiting tales of our beautiful baby...but today?! Already? Is this moment really here? I'm not ready for this yet.

I tell Mike of her presence nearby, and he has the same pained look on his face that I feel in my heart. Are we ready to step into this next phase? I know he feels the same way I do, like I would give anything to be wearing a ridiculous disguise right now. Even one of those funny eyeglass kits with a moustache attached would be a blessing. I revert back to my staring at the ground trick; maybe if I stare down long enough, I will disappear. It must work because she doesn't notice us. We have been spared from this moment...for now. I know that day will come; I know it is headed for us, but I just need a little more time. I think when it happens, when someone who just doesn't know of our last three weeks asks how may baby girl is, I'd like to respond with, "She is a beautiful little angel," and just end the conversation there. After all, it's true. I'm just not sure I can say that yet without tears pouring down my cheeks.

It's strange; throughout my lifetime, the most common compliment I have ever received has always been about my smile. "You have a beautiful smile. You are always smiling. Your smile is contagious, etc." I wonder what my face looks like now. I wonder if when people see me coming into these stores if they think, *What a miserable girl.* I feel like I look mopey and I hate that, but it is how I feel.

I wonder if I'll ever be complimented on my smile ever again. I do hope so. I hope I have the desire to smile a smile again that is worthy of a compliment. I think it will come, especially when I am thinking of Sofie.

Chapter 24

A Tribute to Sofie...

It is bitterly cold this morning—the kind of cold that sinks deep into your bones and causes your body to tremble from within. Appropriately so, today is her funeral.

Sofie's godparents, two of our very best friends, are by our side. The morning begins back at the funeral home, where we will be able to view Sofie's body one last time. I am not nearly as composed today as I was last evening for calling hours. Last evening I became robotic. Countless people came to pay their respects and offer their sympathy. My head was so clouded by the sorrow in my heart that the details are fuzzy at best. I would love to be able to describe what the room looked or smelled like, how it was decorated, or even who was present, but I cannot. Another facet of utter heartbreak is that none of those things mattered. It wouldn't matter if the wallpaper was peeling off the walls or if the ceiling had been made of gold; it all paled in comparison to the resounding pain in my heart.

As each faceless body approached us, my hand extended as if on autopilot. I hugged, kissed, and thanked them for coming. I was a robot.

Today I am not as controlled. I am emotional and raw. Family members force me to sit during the last prayer before we head to the church for the final sendoff. My wavering body is noticeable.

We arrive at the church, and the wind whips through my body. I am directed to process in behind Mike and his brother, Mark, who will carry my baby girl's casket to the front of the church. Their strength is immeasurable. It is not because of her weight or the weight of the pearled, white casket lined with pink satin but because they have the emotional strength to proudly carry her through this moment. I do not. Sofie's godparents walk on either side of me, helping to support my feeble frame. I don't recall the aisle of this church being so endless, so lonely. My tears pave the way for my footsteps, each click of my heels echoing in the somber church.

Father Kraker greets all who have gathered to celebrate Sofie. His words throughout the service are carefully selected and poignant. He speaks of God choosing the most beautiful blooms for his heavenly kingdom. He is trying so hard to offer any sense of comfort during this horrific moment. There are no words to offer such a thing.

Mike is literally holding me up as I am exploding with tears, and just then a wave of warmth rushes over me as Father Kraker begins to sing. Goosebumps line my arms as I recognize the familiar tune. It is Judy Garland's "Somewhere Over the Rainbow." I'm pretty sure there was not a dry eye left in that church as he sang for Sofie.

As the mass concluded, I found strength, once again, to do what Sofie deserved. As her daddy stood strongly by my side, thanking everyone for their support, I began my tribute to Sofie.

Two thousand three hundred and forty-nine; that is a really big number for a twenty-one-day-old. Two thousand three hundred and forty-nine.

My sweet, sweet baby girl, four weeks ago we thought we had everything figured out as we prepared to welcome you to our world. Every last detail was considered: outfits for your hospital pictures, including a variety of hair bows because we weren't sure which one would be perfect enough for you. We were armed with an iPhone, a brand new camera, a video camera, and an extra-large box of batteries because we wanted to be sure that we could capture every moment of your arrival. We had blankets for you to use that we could take home for your puppy dogs to smell so they could learn your scent before we excitedly took you home.

Even my Facebook status was pre-programmed into my phone to announce your beautiful arrival. It was to read, "When I see your face, there's not a thing that I would change because you're amazing just the way you are. *Welcome, Sofia Isabella.*" But we never got that far, did we, baby girl?

Instead I traded neatly pedicured toes for feet that were swollen four times their size as we stood at your crib side, unable to touch you for the first three days of your life. We traded cute post-pregnancy outfits for the quickest three-minute showers and same three outfits that were worn for twenty-one days so we wouldn't have to go home and leave you for a minute longer than necessary. We traded your soft, pretty newborn clothing for a freezing cold cap on your head, EEG leads, hard tubes, and wires. Your warm and cozy nursery was traded for an unfamiliar hospital room with a very different type of monitor displaying every heartbeat and your every breath.

All of our planning certainly never included this—two thousand three hundred and forty-nine.

Life as I had known and planned it completely changed. In my most desperate moments, I prayed unceasingly for a miracle. It took the words of my fifteen-year-old niece for me to realize that you, sweet Sofie…you *are* the miracle. Two thousand three hundred and forty-nine.

Your daddy said it best: "Sofie, you have touched the lives and hearts of so many." You have instilled a sense of faith and love in people across the globe that is immeasurable.

Someone wrote you a message in one of your books that reads, "Sofia, the world is singing of the wonder of you." And it is. Two thousand three hundred and forty-nine.

From Japan, Germany, India, Argentina, Australia, New Zealand, Canada, and across every state in the United States, there are people praying for, thinking about, inspired by, and loving you.

You have changed the way people look at life, the way they believe, and the way that they love. You have brought people back to their faith. *You*, our precious eight-pound, beautiful girl, have impacted hundreds.

Our sweet, sweet baby girl, who was never able to open her eyes, has taught hundreds of people how to see differently. Our little baby girl whose tiny voice we never got to hear utter a single cry spoke loudly to hundreds of hearts. Your daddy beamed as he said, "How many other twenty-one-day-olds can claim that? I am so proud of her."

And we are. We are so proud of how strong you showed us you could be when you shouldn't have had to. We are so proud of the love you created that swept the globe, capturing the hearts of everyone who learned about you. I would receive message after message from people who would begin, "You don't know me. I am a friend of a friend of a friend who knows you, but here is how Sofia has changed my life." How could we not be proud?

We are so proud of you, baby girl. We are so proud to be your mama and daddy.

You Sofie, *are* a miracle. Two thousand three hundred and forty-nine—the number of messages and cards of prayers, thoughts, and love that you received in just twenty-one days, a short yet powerful life.

One of those messages we received read, "Sofia Isabella, it's the name that sings itself." It is, baby girl, and the world will continue to sing your sweet song.

One of our favorite books that we read to you begins, "On the night you were born, the moon smiled with such wonder that the stars peeked in to see you, and the night wind whispered…life will never be the same."

Our world has been changed forever because of you. You are the living example that, "There is no footprint too small to leave an imprint on the world." Two thousand three hundred and forty-nine messages of love to you confirm that.

While our time together has been much too short, while you've had to endure more than any newborn baby girl should ever have to, we have cherished every minute with you. We will cherish every moment that we got to hold you, see your face, peek inside of those big blue eyes, and stroke your soft, soft skin and silky hair. The memory of holding you close against me and feeling you breathe against my skin will forever bring me peace.

I loved the tender moments we shared together with Daddy, though they weren't at all as we had planned.

Sofie, while our time together on this earth was not nearly long enough for your daddy or me, and while there is nothing right about being here in this church for this reason today, we would do it all over again just to have the moments we had with you. You are in my heart forever, baby girl; you are the best part of me.

I now live for the day when I am going about my daily routine and someone hears or sees my name and stops to ask me if I am related to *the* Sofia Dente who changed the world. I will look at them proudly, with a big smile on my face as I proclaim, "I am her mom."

When we were in the hospital, Daddy picked a book that quickly became our favorite. We believe it became your favorite as well. We never left your room for the night, no matter how late it was, before reading it to you as we tucked you in. I hope you all don't mind as we read this to our baby girl today before she is laid to her final place of rest.

Sweet pea, our very own Little Nut Brown Hare, Mama and Daddy will always love you right up to the moon and back. We love you so much, baby girl. As the chocolate, brown scrolled decal on your perfectly pink nursery wall above your crib reads, "Sweetest Dreams, Tiny One."

The reading of *Guess How Much I Love You?* by Sam McBratney concluded her service, her final goodnight story.

91

I hope you do find people you can be not-awkward with. As for me, I'd be happy to come over and throw fruit with you. Take that, you damn fruit baskets!

—CLAIRE WHITE, A GOOD FRIEND

CHAPTER 25

THE FIRST DAY OF THE REST OF OUR LIVES...

The plans are completed, the ceremonies are finished, and the last of the guests have left. Today Mike and I feebly begin our new lives. I have a love-hate relationship already with this new life. I mostly hate it. I didn't ask for this life. Our lives had always been so drama-free. We both have good jobs, we get along well, and we have a nice house and great friends and family. I don't know how things changed for us so quickly. I didn't ask for this life, and I certainly don't want it. I want the life we should have had.

I sit in Sofia's nursery and look around at her tastefully, created room. Her light pink walls in a shade called "Be Mine" that took hours to pick out to be sure that we got it just right now stare emptily at me. The hand-painted by Daddy dark brown letters that echo Sofia's beautiful name, which were hung with such care and concern to ensure that each letter was precisely equidistant from the last, now hang depressingly over a gorgeous changing table/dresser that will no longer be used.

The closet is filled with an array of amazing clothes that speak of the future we should have had, including dresses for upcoming weddings, bathing suits for her first beach trip, and even a pair of cowgirl boots for her first trip to Texas to meet her Papa and Grammy—beautiful clothes Sofie will never wear. I keep trying to convince myself and almost believe that somehow, some way, Sofie will be coming back. But she's not. I hate this life.

But I can't hate all of it because it does include Sofie. She was here and is the best part of both of my lives, the former and this current life that I hate. I can't deny or denounce this new life completely because I would never deny or denounce her—her beauty, her significance, her life, or my love for her. But I do hate this new life that doesn't physically include her by my side.

I feel like I am in a bubble, desperately pushing, punching, and kicking the walls to break through but I am unable, and it feels suffocating. Why can't I get out of this? Why can't I break free? Why can't I just wake up from this?!? Yup…I am back to that.

I tell my best friend that it is getting harder and harder every morning when I wake up to hope that this has all just been a horrible nightmare and harder to believe that I may still be able to find a way to wake up from this. Maybe tomorrow morning?

I hate this life. Mike and I clean and organize. It's amazing how one life can fit so neatly into a couple of decorative boxes. I received the flowers, pictures, and items from the funeral home today. I stare at their stunning photo creation of our family. An entire lifetime captured in one little collage. It makes me sad. I am so sad that we don't have a lifetime to create new collages with Sof.

I hate this new life. Mike and I discuss being a part of this new, disgusting club and how it feels like we have been branded, that we will forever feel like we are the equivalent of walking around in public completely naked. Everyone knows that we are different, that we have been changed; we are the new elephants in the room.

This situation is terrible, completely shitty, if you don't mind. It is tragic and awful, but it doesn't have to be awkward. It is so many bad things, but awkward it will not be.

Our daughter's life was not awkward, her being born was not awkward, and our love for her is not awkward. The situation is terrible, but it should not be awkward.

It was so calming, comforting, and healing to have my two closest friends staying with us for Sofie's services. I admit I didn't want to have that initially. I wanted to hole away during this time and interact with people as little as possible, giving me as much time as I wanted to hide under my blankets and cry. Mike convinced me to have them stay with us, and I am forever grateful that he knows me better than I know myself right now.

I needed them to be with us. Together we shared moments of joy over Sofie, moments of anger and tears regarding the outcome, and then moments of complete normalcy. We were able to find an amazing balance between regular conversations and then weave naturally back to conversations about Sofie, about what she should have had, and then back again to topics of normal adults who haven't just been stricken with the deepest tragedy of their lives.

I want to always be able to discuss Sofie's life as well as discuss her in the present. I want people to know about our daughter and not have it be awkward just because of the shitty hand we have been dealt. We are still Mike and Lori, not Mike and Lori, the unfortunate parents of a baby who died. We are Mike and Lori, the parents of a beautiful baby girl who happened to be with us for too short of a time. Are we different because of her? Yes. Are we broken right now? Yes. Do we need to learn how to exist in this new life we have found ourselves in? Yes. Are we too fragile to discuss certain things around? No. Are we too sad to talk about our experience or our daughter? No.

This situation sucks, but the only thing that could make any of this even worse is for it to feel awkward. We have invited so many on this journey with us from the minute I announced my pregnancy so loudly and joyously, and that journey was so welcomed by so many. This outcome could not have been predicted, and it is terribly unfair.

You have all been invited to share in Sofie's life and invited to sit with me in my grief—in all of our grief. Sit with me in this crappy situation, please. Let it be tragic at times, sad at times, joy-filled at times, unfair at times, but never, never awkward.

And now, for the rest of tonight, I head back to my blankets to hide and cry. I miss you terribly, sweet pea.

I just want her back.

—*Facebook status update: February 22, 2011*

Chapter 26

A Harsh Dose of Reality...

Sleeping has become my double-edged sword. I love going to sleep at night because it's the only time my brain is able to stop running in circles of a future I am uncertain and terrified of. When I sleep, my brain sleeps. It is also the only time I may have a chance of seeing, holding, hearing, or touching my sweet baby girl.

I would sleep all day if I could because waking up is absolutely awful. Waking up throttles me back into this life that I do not want.

This morning when I wake, the house is quiet...so quiet. I crumble out of bed. Last night before I went to sleep, I cried to Sofie. I told her, "Mama will be strong tomorrow. You don't have to give Mama any signs that you are OK because Daddy is going to need you to be extra close to him. So please, Sof, look after him tomorrow. Mama will be OK."

Mike has returned to work today. This is the first day in a month that he has been away from me for more than a couple of hours. I

97

used to be independent; hell, I prided myself on that. Mike and I are great together, but we have also always been great when we are apart.

This is just another thing that has been stripped from me. I suddenly am very aware that I am alone today. I feel like a child who has been left home alone for the first time ever. Though I'm not afraid of the house catching on fire, someone strange coming to the door, or the phone ringing and having to tell someone that my parents aren't at home; I'm simply afraid of myself. I am afraid to be left alone with my thoughts and this brain that will not stop.

Then the harsher reality strikes. This is my maternity leave. This is the time I have been eagerly awaiting for months. This is the time I have been anticipating and preparing for. It is here, but I have no baby to share it with.

My morning should not begin with sleeping in, leisurely cups of coffee, and trying to figure out how I am going to fill this day to distract myself from complete sobbing episodes. My morning should begin with being jolted awake by my Sofie's screams to let me know she is hungry or wet or both. I should be trying to find five minutes to take a shower, feeling overwhelmed as I try to manage her routine and the two dogs, all while trying to keep the house somewhat clean. I should be much too busy to be writing this but managing to find time to gush over and publically share her newest picture of the day, capturing her continued growth and new developments as she transforms into the little girl she will become.

But this is it. Welcome to your maternity leave, minus the baby. It is just so quiet.

The morning is a rough one filled with a lot of tears and occasional yelling and screaming at the walls because it doesn't feel like God is listening. I almost break down and beg Sofie for a sign that she is OK. But I remember my promise to her last night; I will find the strength so she can be with Mike today.

I shower…barely, and pull myself together long enough to get dressed because my sister-in-law is coming over in about fifteen minutes. I am embarrassed that she could have potentially arrived during my screaming at the walls rant, but luckily she did not, though I know she would have understood and maybe would have even joined me.

I almost cancelled on her today but once again am thankful that I did not. I can't imagine an entire day of yelling at the walls, and sadly I know that is exactly where my day was headed.

My distraction arrives. Together we cry, talk, tidy the house, and hang some amazing pictures of Sofie. She takes me to the grocery store so I won't have to go alone. I suddenly understand how my grandmother must have felt after my grandfather died. She was older, in her seventies, but she relied on him for everything. She never drove, only occasionally worked, and did nothing without him. I feel like a weak old woman who requires assistance to function at such a basic level. It feels strange to lose my independence, but I have. If she was not with me, I would not have ventured out into this suddenly enormous and terrifying world.

I do OK at the grocery store until we wait in line to check out. I feel like a sitting duck. There is too much opportunity to run into someone who doesn't know what happened or worse…someone who does. It feels awful.

I start to well up as I look at our empty shopping cart. It is filled with food but still so empty. I am reminded of a shower gift that we received, a shopping cart cover, so simple yet suddenly so meaningful. The shopping cart cover is pink and girly, and now it sits in my closet and will never be used by Sofie. I have had plenty of moments grieving the dreams I've had for Sofie, for Mike and myself, but it's these little everyday moments that truly sting. Sofie should be with me at the grocery store. All of these mundane tasks should be that much brighter because she is with me. But she's not. She will never use that pink shopping cart cover, and I hate that.

My outing ends when we bring Sofie some new flowers. I have survived another day, almost. I do still have the rest of the night. I think Mike is planning to work from home tomorrow, so maybe, Sof, maybe I can have that sign tomorrow. I love you, sweet pea.

CHAPTER 27

A HAPPY ONE-MONTH NOTE TO SOFIE...

It's hard to believe that our entire world changed one month ago today. Happy one-month mark, my sweet girl.

I do wish you were here with us to celebrate, and celebrate we would do! I wish I could have scooped you out of your crib this morning and given you the biggest happy one month kiss! We would have picked a stunning outfit to take a joyous picture in to post for all to see.

I wonder how you would be growing; who you would look more like today? I wonder what new and wondrous things we would be noticing in you that you weren't doing a few weeks ago.

It is a special day, and I'm just so sad we don't get to share it in that way.

Instead I went into your nursery, sat on your floor without you, and read you a book. I missed cradling you and caressing your soft skin as I read, but I know you heard it.

Even if not the way we had hoped or planned, we still celebrate you because you do live on. We will celebrate you today on your one-month anniversary, and we will celebrate you tomorrow. We will celebrate you on a random Tuesday and Friday and Sunday; we will celebrate you every day.

We did receive the most outstanding one-month gift for you in the mail today. It was a song written for you, Mama, and Daddy. It was written using the words we spoke to you on the night you were freed from all of those hard tubes—from all of your struggles. It was an amazing surprise to honor your special day.

Tonight we went to dinner with Aunt Cathy, Aunt Judy, Uncle Jim, and Lizzy. It wasn't easy, but I promised you as I got dressed that we were celebrating you, and it gave my evening purpose. You give my life purpose.

I thought of you the entire night, even when I was conversing about something different. I suppose this is how the rest of my life will be, talking and doing other things but constantly thinking of you… and that, my dear girl, is not a bad thing.

Daddy and I toasted to your one month. Someone wrote to me tonight, "Enjoy a moment each day…somehow." There are many moments throughout the day spent thinking of you, loving you, celebrating you that are easy to enjoy. It is just the ones in between that bring such sorrow because we want to be enjoying these moments with you in such a different way.

But I promise you, sweet pea, it will never be too hard to find a moment each day to enjoy you. Happy one month, baby girl. I love you.

I am waiting for my plague of locusts.

—*Facebook status update: March 1, 2011*

CHAPTER 28

RAINY DAYS AND SUNDAYS ALWAYS GET ME DOWN...

Warning...this chapter in my new life is not for the faint of heart. It is not intended for those who offend easily and may disappoint those who have held on to the illusion of my strong faith through this process. Proceed with caution...

Sunday mornings in particular seem a little extra cruel. I haven't been able to pinpoint the exact logic or reasoning for this. Maybe it's because it marks the last day of the weekend when Mike will be home with me before the next day catapults me, without my consent, into another week of being by myself in which I have to fight day after day for survival.

I feel like I am in some new, bizarre, and incredibly harsh reality game show. (Insert booming movie voice here.) "Will Lori survive twenty-four hours of painstaking, gut-wrenching heartache as she is relentlessly reminded of the life she should have had? Will she crawl her way out of the cavern of doom and emptiness (spoken, of course with a resounding echo effect) disguised as a perfectly decorated nursery topped off with a closet full of beautiful clothes for upcoming special events that her baby girl will not be attending!?" It is a sick, sick reality show.

Maybe Sundays are hard because they use to mark easy, breezy days of relaxing family time, and now our lives are as far from that description as humanly and literally possible.

The Sunday after Sofie's services is no different. One week ago today, we were encompassed by family, friends, and loved ones who came to honor the little girl who touched so many hearts. It was a long and draining day, but I could look to my left and see my precious girl. I would never have thought through any of this that I would have found comfort in that moment. I would never have thought that looking over to my left and seeing my baby girl in her casket would bring a peace that I will later yearn for because I will never see her body again.

I could walk over and kiss her cold, hard cheek that felt more like a wooden doll than her soft, inviting skin used to before she was prepared. I could comb my fingers through her soft, silky hair and gently tap the tip of her tiny button nose. But today, this Sunday, I have nothing.

I realize I'm awake before I open my eyes, and I don't want to open them. I don't want to move because I'm afraid I'll touch my stomach and realize I am no longer pregnant and once again will be thrust into facing this reality that I so hate.

Another habit I have formed in this new life is developing a carnal, grunting sigh that comes out when there are simply no words to express the pain and sadness I feel. When some moments just seem too much to bear, when I realize again that she is not here and is not coming back, I can only muster this primal noise.

So on this Sunday morning, as I slowly peel my eyelids apart, I grunt and sigh. As quickly as I am awakened from my slumber, the thoughts of what have happened to us in these past weeks come flooding into my mind before I even stand a chance to close the reality reminder gates.

Like a tsunami they flood me, relentlessly crashing against my heart with no consideration for its open wounds. I try to swim, but I can't fight the vigorous current. It is too forceful; I am too weak. Before I realize it, I am drowning, drowning in these thoughts of what ifs, if onlys, whys, and hows. There is no rescue team in this scenario; there are no life preservers, only a giant boatload of guilt. The flooding gush of thoughts must be too much for my heart and brain because there they come, pouring out of my eyes.

There I am, barely awake two minutes, and I am engulfed in tears and retching cries. Mike swiftly turns around to see what has happened. As I explain my tears, he sharply reminds me, "You did nothing wrong. You need to stop going back to that place. There is nothing we can do to change the outcome." I sense a frustration from him that I keep regressing to this place. I admire his ability to not replay the same scenarios thousands of times. I don't *want* to continue to play these awful mind games in which I always lose, but I can't stop. I don't know how to. No one can tell me how to.

He goes to shower for church this morning. I remain in my dark place alone. I slowly get myself showered and dressed to attend church with him. I don't want to go; I don't feel ready.

One night during one of those late-night chats with Sofie, I promised her I would go to church every week with Daddy because I knew it would be important to him. I told her I would not go for any other reason but to use that hour to think of her. "Daddy has been so strong for your mama; the least I can do is stand by his side at church." So on this morning, as weak as I feel, I will go and stand with Mike.

We arrive to the church and sit down. It's too soon, not even a week since we sat here for our baby girl's funeral. I begin to cry. My eyes are filled with tears as the service begins, but I can make out Father Kraker's compassionate face as he walks down the aisle. He spots me and offers a soft head nod that appears to say, "I know this is hard, but I'm glad to see you."

I try to draw strength from anything, but all I can see are my own tears, hovering in my eyes. Father Kraker begins by having everyone offer a "good morning" to those seated around them. Ugh, today, of all days? It's so obvious that I am crying; I imagine these people around me are wondering, *What is wrong with her?*

I just want to hide; I want to be invisible. I quickly hang my head down with my chin pressed against my chest. No eye contact is made with anyone, and I utter no words. I turn my entire body toward Mike, like a shy child about to meet someone new, and wait for this moment to pass. Mike warmly greets those around us. I envy him and I'm angry all at the same time. How is this so easy for him? Deep down, I know it's not.

The first reading begins: "Can a mother forget her infant, be without tenderness for the child of her womb? Even should she forget, I will never forget you" (Isaiah. 49:1).

I simply can't handle this…at all. I find myself crying uncontrollably in the pew. I get up and run across the aisle, through the entire church toward the restroom as I sob. I wish I could say that no one noticed me, but there was nothing inconspicuous about my abrupt exit. Really? Six days after we bury our daughter, who we wanted more than anything in our entire lives, and this is the first reading today?

I later share this difficult experience with my sister, Lisa. She works as chaplain and has always maintained a strong faith throughout her life. She gently suggests that this reading that tugged at my heart so much was perhaps intended for comfort. That even with my understanding of how a mother could never forget the child in her womb and the new appreciation for that bond I have, God is saying that even if a woman *could* forget or be without that child, He never will.

"He will never forget or forsake, Sofie."

I bitterly respond, "Well then God should have known I wouldn't have been ready to handle that reading just yet."

Let me shed some light on some of the cause of my anger and hurt toward God, other than the obvious.

After having our early miscarriage last year and having difficulty conceiving at all, the moment we learned of Sofie's pregnancy, I took nothing for granted. Week after week at church for nine months, the one and *only* thing I ever prayed for was for Sofie to be healthy and happy and that the three of us would live long lives together. That is it…that was the silent intention in my heart that I prayed for repetitively every week as I stood in this very church.

When I was in Italy at six weeks pregnant, we altered our plans to remain in Rome on a Sunday to attend a blessing by the pope at St. Peter's Square. As he leaned out the window to bless the crowd, in all of my naïve amazement, my prayer remained the same.

During difficult days at work, after supporting a family who was faced with making the decision to remove their own baby from life support, I would retreat to my office and say aloud to Sofie and God, "May we never have to know what this family is going through."

I was so aware and thankful of how blessed I was in those moments as I prepared to welcome my healthy baby girl into our lives.

Why did I even waste my breath? How did I become so forsaken by God? How did Sofie? It's not like I went about my days being ignorant to all I had and all I was expecting. I never took for granted the miracle of life after experiencing a miscarriage. I never took for granted that I was healthy, and I had genuine empathy and compassion for the difficult situations so many families I worked with were forced to face. I never thought, *Better them than me,* but rather, *God, how lucky are we that we are not in their shoes, and may we **never** have to know what that feels like.*

What was God doing through all of this? With His all-knowing, powerful self, was He listening to my words and laughing because I had absolutely no idea how ironic this was all about to become? Did He decide I was just too pompous living a life void of sadness and that I deserved to be knocked down a few notches?

And now, as I sit in "His house" for the first time since my daughter's funeral, hanging on by a thread, I am greeted with a reading that elicits a feeling of abandonment of a mother toward her child. Trust me, I didn't need the help of a Bible verse to elicit such a feeling; I already feel like I have failed as a mother all on my own.

I compose myself as much as possible, which isn't very good at all, and do a walk of shame back through the church to my seat. I make eye contact with no one, though I'm pretty sure no one wanted to make eye contact with me either.

It is time for the collection; of course let's give money to this whole establishment that I doubt so much these days. I look up; the gentleman passing the basket is none other than our funeral director for Sofie's services. Are you kidding me, God!? As he nears, he recognizes me; his face softens, saddens, and he leans down and hugs me. I lose control of my tears once again. I can't handle this. I am too weak. Does this all-knowing God not understand this, or is this just part of the joke?

I try to regain some sense of myself as I sit next to Mike, who I am sure is completely embarrassed by my emotional outpouring. I refuse to actively participate in the service at all. I will not make the sign of the cross out of pure rebellion. I occasionally find myself accidentally repeating the prayers silently in my head, and I angrily reprimand myself. I will not say the prayers. Who is listening anyway? I sit and stare angrily ahead, as if in a staring contest with God Himself.

It's time for communion. Finally this is almost over. But before I can ride out the remainder of the service, the communion hymn begins. It is a full choir singing "Amazing Grace," the entrance hymn for Sofie's funeral. I cannot tell you the last time this song was played during a regular mass at this church. I truly want to die. I don't even try to hide my tears anymore; I just need this to be over, to get out of this suffocation of painful reminders in a place that is supposed to offer peace. Yeah right.

We beeline out of the church. Mike is walking briskly ahead of me, out of sheer embarrassment I'm sure. I have never been so happy to return home to my safe zone. I curl up on the couch. God: one. Lori: zero.

The next morning, Mike returns to work. I hate this. Another freaking awesome day of maternity leave all alone.

It is a rainy, gloomy morning, an exact match of my mood. I head downstairs and immediately step into a wet spot on our carpet barefooted. Awesome, the dog must have had an accident; a fabulous start to this day. As I attempt to clean it, I walk across the living room only to notice the carpet here is also damp. There is no way the dog had an accident here too. I call Mike. This is strange.

He explains that last night during torrential storms, our dog refused to come in and got soaked, so she slept downstairs; that must be why it's wet. It doesn't make sense to me; there is no trail of wetness that she would have tracked in. After further discussion, he remembers that there is a drain under our carpet, behind the couch. He wonders if with all of this heavy rain, water is getting in. I move the couch, and we have our answer. Our basement is being soaked with water pouring in from under the wall.

If nothing else, I have a project to distract me today. I follow his suggestion and go purchase a shop vac. I come home, frustratingly put it together, and get to work. I have never used a shop vac, and I have no idea what I am doing. I return to the site of the water and realize in the short time I was gone, the amount of carpet that is wet has tripled. I place the shop vac hose at the site of the water entry. I wait about two minutes and wonder if I even put it together correctly. I don't think it's doing anything. I open the lid to peek in, and to my surprise, it is already full. Uh-oh. Fourteen gallons full, and no difference made on our carpet. This is bad.

I roll the bucket toward our stairs. I guess in my new fuzzy-headed state, I never considered that fourteen gallons of water would be heavy and even heavier for someone who is still recovering from a delivery and hasn't used abdominal muscles in ten months. I try to lug the bucket up our stairs to dump it out the front door. I can't do it. I refuse to give up. I mean, my God, I have to be able to do something right or have something work out the way it is supposed to! I try again and again; I begin to slowly make progress, one step at a time. I reach the halfway point, and the unthinkable happens. The lid pops off, and the entire fourteen gallons of water spills on the other half of our finished basement, the only half that had remained dry.

When the lid to that shop vac popped off, so did any restraint I had on my self-control. I start screaming at the top of my lungs, and my poor dogs seek shelter to avoid my wrath.

As loud as my vocal cords will allow, I scream at God, "I hate You so much!" I repeat it is countless times, "I hate You! I have never hated the way that I hate You!" My entire self is shaking vigorously as the hate for Him exudes from every pore in body. I burst into pure rage. "I don't understand why You have forsaken me so much and so easily! Why does this whole universe hate me?"

I scream to Him as I recall the Bible story of the prodigal son. An entire story based on the love and joy of the homecoming of a child who returns after choosing to leave his father. The one-way screaming match continues. "I didn't choose to leave! You abandoned me!" The screaming statements of hate are peppered with colorful language that I will spare all of you. It's language that I'm sure would mortify Christians every-where, let alone the fact that I am directing it to God Himself.

I am recalling that same Bible story. The father is overjoyed when his son finally returns, welcoming him with no questions, only love. "I didn't walk away from You! You left me! I don't understand why You wouldn't even try to keep me!"

Between Sofie's unexpected injury that led to her death, the slap in the face service yesterday, and now this, why does He feel the need to spiritually kick me when I am already so down, broken, and bleeding from every possible orifice? It is already not a fair fight. I have *no* control and yet, "You, You have all control, and all You do is wound me!" I scream at Him for hours; my throat is hoarse. I am so angry, so bitter, and yet so hurt. I collapse into tears of sadness and betrayal.

I don't understand why He has abandoned me. I have worked for the church in my life. I have excitedly talked with others about faith, hope, and the love of God. I have lived my life as a Christian, and even in my profession I strive to help others. I am hurt that He has so easily thrown me to the wayside and doesn't appear to care at all. He refused to protect Sofie in those last days of pregnancy; He refused to grant us the miracle that literally hundreds of people were praying for. He refused to grant my prayer of nine months for a happy, healthy Sofie. I hate Him more than I've ever hated anything. I hate Him for casting me aside so carelessly like I never mattered at all. I hate Him for taking my sweet girl away from us. I hate Him!

The flood continues to ravage our basement. I am able to rely on supportive friends, family, and an incredible fire department that comes to assist. Sofie's Uncle Mark rushes over the moment he learns of today's events, and Mike comes home from work early. We manage to save our furniture and all of Sofie's items that were downstairs.

All that is lost is our flooring, and we can replace that for an expense. It's an expense we don't need right now with funeral home bills, medical bills, and the future bill of purchasing a headstone, but we will manage.

As this atrocious day comes to an end, my faith is restored in the kindness and generosity of people. That is all, just in the people around me, and today that is the *only* place where my faith lies.

I think Sof is just too little to be this far away from home this late at night.

—F*ACEBOOK STATUS UPDATE*: M*ARCH* 16, 2011

CHAPTER 29

BEWARE THE EIGHTEENTH OF MARCH...

Today is a bittersweet day. Well, really I guess it's bittersweet minus the sweet, just as most days seem to be. Today is March 18th. This day should be seemingly benign. It isn't a birthday, a death day, the day we found out we were pregnant—nothing like that. It should be a harmless Friday, but it's not. Today is our local school district's reverse raffle. We attend every year along with the rest of our town to benefit local sports' programs.

The reverse raffle is the place where I met Mike's family for the first time and hopefully won their stamp of approval. We had just been dating four weeks, and it was magnificent. An easy evening full of laughter, joy, and excitement as I got a glimpse into the future that would later be mine with this loving family.

Months ago, when the date of the reverse raffle was announced Mike mentioned us going. I laughed, snarked, if you will. "I'm not going to be ready to leave her home for a night out that soon."

My friend Amy giggled at my naivety. "I have babysat for friends' babies at three weeks old. You'll be fine." I knew I would be fine, but I just didn't think I'd *want* to leave her just yet. But Mike convinced me that it would be a nice trial run to ease myself into the reality of leaving her in daycare three days per week.

So months ago, Friday March 18th, became no longer benign. It marks the first night Mike and I planned to go out and leave our baby girl with a babysitter for the first time. The babysitter was booked and ready to go—Sofie's cousin Lizzy, who is more like her big sister and was so excited to watch her.

I had it all figured out. I'd feed her, get her down for a bit, be at the raffle for a few hours, and then be back home as soon as possible to pick up where I left off. It wouldn't be easy to pry myself away from her, but she wouldn't even realize we'd been gone. And of course, I'd just call and check in every thirty minutes or so.

There's only one thing missing for my plan to go off without a hitch: Sofie.

Tonight, March 18th, I get ready for the reverse raffle. I have no trouble getting showered or dressed because there is no baby requiring my attention. Mike and I leave our silent, dark, empty house without a babysitter and head out. This night was so different than I had planned, yet still I am sad and aching for her. That part I know would have felt the same had she been here.

We arrive to the doors as I walk slightly behind Mike, the entire time just repeating, "This is so weird, this is just so weird." As we open the doors and stand in line, my flight response kicks in. I just want to go home.

It's too late; a familiar face spots us, shakes Mike's hand, and nods empathetically to me. He says it is good to see us and that he is sorry for our loss. It is very kind of him, yet I feel branded. I feel like everyone in this line knows our sad story and is whispering behind our back about our dead baby. I think they must dread talking to us for fear they will catch what we have and their own children will be in jeopardy. I'm sure this is not the case, but man does it feel like that.

To my surprise, it doesn't take long to blend into the crowd, to just mindlessly participate in the night's events, and that too is difficult. Suddenly we are not recognized at all, not recognized as the couple whose baby just died, not recognized as a branded, sad, downtrodden pair but also not recognized as Sofia's mom and dad, and that is terrible too.

I don't understand the need for the extremes. One minute I am feeling like I am wearing a bright scarlet "DB" on my chest and the next minute I am drowning in the anonymity. It is awful to not know what you want or need, and I don't…oh wait, yes I do. I want and need my daughter to be back with me and restored to health the way it should have been. Until then, I float between the extremes.

The night continues. I catch myself checking my phone incessantly to make sure I didn't miss a call from the babysitter; you know, the call that will never come, but I can't stop myself.

We talk about Sofie a lot tonight just about every chance we get. I can almost feel people becoming exhausted with our ongoing discussion of her, or maybe it's this paranoid state I have found myself in these days.

Our reverse raffle number is Sofie's birthday. I joke that we will likely be the first ones out given our ridiculous turn of recent events. Then I remember that the first people out still win a small prize, so we'll probably be the second number called. We aren't. We don't win either, but at least we hung in there for a while, just like our baby girl.

The night comes to a close, and Mike and I head home. My eyes fill with tears as we climb into bed, with only our dogs to take care of for the night. March 18th is almost over, thankfully.

Dear little girl carrying the Barbie doll at the gym, I'm sorry that when you saw me look at you and smile and you asked me my name that my response was filled with tears in my eyes. I did not intend to freak you out or become that scary lady at the gym.

—FACEBOOK STATUS UPDATE: MARCH 25

CHAPTER 30

A WORKOUT FOR THE HEART…

The universe being the universe doesn't cut slack in areas of your life when other areas have gone so tragically wrong; this I have learned. How else could you explain not only *not* having my baby girl here with me tonight to rock to sleep, kiss her soft little head, smell her sweet scent, or just look over at her sleeping nestled closely on her daddy's chest? (This list could go on and on, but I think I would probably lose the interest of those reading.) But in the face of losing Sofie so tragically, I also still have the physical aspects of having been pregnant for nine months attached tightly to my stomach and thighs. It is just wrong. Not only have I been left infant-less, sad, and broken but also flabby. Ugh.

I have been limiting most of my workouts to long walks with the dogs around the block, walking briskly not only to try to regain some muscle tone but mostly to avoid anyone stopping me along the way who may ask about my new baby.

Tonight I decided to brace myself and head to the gym with Mike. Even under normal circumstances in my old life, I dreaded the gym. I was never one of those people who would feel better having gone, like my sister. After working out she'd always ask, "Aren't you so glad you went? Don't you feel better now?" My answer, always a very confident no.

I hate the smell, I hate the physical exertion, and I hate the other people seemingly watching me and judging how slow I am running or noting that I wasn't on that machine nearly long enough. OK, that may be a little narcissistic.

First we stop to visit Sof and bring her some very cool solar-powered butterfly stakes picked out by her daddy. Now all night she will have two beautiful butterflies exuding their soothing glow of reds, blues, yellows, and greens. They are perfect for her, and every baby girl needs a night-light.

Then we get there; the gym. I do hate it so, but I also know I would really like to unfriend these last few pounds that have become all too attached to me. I walk in and am surprised that I even remember my code to sign in. (It has been a long time.) I wonder if when my picture pops up and the kind attendant reviews it, if she'll think, *Wow has she aged*.

I book it for the locker room and pick the first empty locker I spot. I look at the combination that was left on the lock from the last user; it is Sofie's birthday. Weird.

To my surprise, I somewhat enjoy working out. It feels good to physically push myself to release some of my stress, my anger…my grief.

I finish a respectable workout and find Mike; he is an avid gym goer and excels athletically, especially compared to me. He isn't even close to being done. I decide to walk on the track until he finishes.

I go upstairs with my iPod and walk away. I forgot I had our song on my pod, "Just the Way You Are" by Bruno Mars, the one Sofie would come alive with in utero every time it played. It makes me smile as I see flashes of her in my mind. I recall all of our tender little moments, her stretches, the way she felt when I held her, and of course the scoop and swoop—the move that myself and the nurses perfected for picking Sofie up while popping her off the vent. I did become an expert in the scoop and swoop, if I do say so myself.

116

But then it finds me, like that person you recognize at the grocery store the one time you go wearing sweats and no makeup. You hope they won't see you, but then all of a sudden you turn the corner and smack right into their cart. Yup, that's what it's like. Grief—the unwanted encounter. I start to cry. I continue to walk around the track, hoping that if I walk quickly maybe people will think my tears are beads of sweat from a really, really good workout. I don't think I fooled anyone. I certainly didn't fool myself.

I exit the track and lay down to stretch. I lay down, staring at the bright lights on the ceiling. I am so empty. How did our lives get so off track? How did Sofie never get a chance to really live? I recall my plan to take Sofie to the gym to walk this very track with her stroller as I had seen so many new moms do before. I miss her. I miss not being able to share every moment with her, be it at home, at the grocery store, or even at the dreaded gym.

I lose track of time staring into space, and my iPod plays in its random order. I have so many songs on there that I rarely listen to. I am struck by the beautiful voice in a song from the musical *Wicked* that starts to play. I love this musical and forgot I had put this music on my iPod. I have run to "Defying Gravity" many a time, and it gave me inspiration for my first four-mile race with Mike a couple of years ago. So many fun and lively songs…but this one is different. It is slow, captivating, haunting. The words touch me:

I've heard it said
That people come into our lives for a reason
Bringing something we must learn
And we are led
To those who help us most to grow
If we let them
And we help them in return
Well, I don't know if I believe that's true
But I know I'm who I am today
Because I knew you…
Who can say if I've been changed for the better?
But because I knew you
I have been changed for good

It well may be
That we will never meet again
In this lifetime
So let me say before we part
So much of me
Is made of what I learned from you
You'll be with me
Like a handprint on my heart
And now whatever way our stories end
I know you have rewritten mine… (Stephen Schwartz)

I wipe my tears away, knowing her handprint has been left on my heart. Whatever way my story now ends, I know Sofie has rewritten mine, and that because I have known and loved her, I have been changed for good. Who would ever have thought that this baby girl who I grew inside of me for forty-plus weeks would really have helped me grow so drastically in such a different and more substantial way?

I miss her terribly, but I love her even more. I suspect there will be more tears tonight as I miss my sweet girl, but I will make sure that every day, regardless of what I am doing, that it is known that all of me "is made of what I learned" from her.

I love you, Sofie, and I hold you close to me in this and every moment. Sweetest dreams, tiny one.

CHAPTER 31

DENYING ACCEPTANCE...

They say there are stages of grief, and I believe it. I think we can all attest to some very clear stages that I have encountered in the course of this journey thus far. I understand that I am not so far removed from the newness of this experience to qualify me as any type of expert in the matter of grief. However, I feel like I can confidently say that there is one stage that I just don't believe applies to the death of your child.

I have been depressed, I have bargained, I think we can all confidently state that I've been angry. Sadly, because of my work experience I think I was slightly robbed of the denial stage, but I can attribute that stage to my unending hope that I will still somehow wake up and have it be January and we will get her out in time. But acceptance—that stage I just can't even believe in.

I understand the stage; I understand that my daughter has died. I understand that our lives are not at all what they were expected to be. I understand that whatever our future brings, our lives will never make sense because she is not here.

I understand that if we should ever be blessed with living siblings of Sof, they will never have the parents they would have had if Sofie had been alive and well. Our lives have been affected and changed forever. A next pregnancy, a next delivery, bringing home healthy siblings (hopefully one day), and raising and parenting siblings while continuing to learn how to parent Sofie will continue to be a new process, different than anything imaginable, with no course book on how to prepare.

I understand that Sofie is not coming back, but I will *never* accept that. I will never accept what happened to her because it simply should never have been. I will never accept that she is gone because she should be here. I will never accept that this is our new life because somehow I feel like that constitutes some sort of compliance on my part, a nodding of my OK that this has happened, and well, that I can confidently say, will just never be.

I am learning how to be the parent to an angel, how to involve her, include her, and learn from her every day. Death does not erase her place in our family. Death does not erase her importance in my life today, tomorrow, or for the rest of my days. It is a process.

Some days I simply hate that parenting my daughter consists of cleaning the dead flowers from her grave. Other days I celebrate being able to parent her by honoring her in a myriad of ways that thankfully seem unending.

I will never accept that Sofie has died; I just don't think I will ever have it in me. No disrespect is intended to those who researched and discovered this stage of grief, but clearly *they* didn't lose *their* baby girl.

All I can do is the best I can as I float in and out of these various stages. I imagine I will continue to bargain, be depressed and sadly angry again at times, and have moments when I just want to deny this has happened at all. But I know in my heart I will work through all of these stages toward a healthier tomorrow as I live to celebrate my baby girl, but I will never, ever accept that she is gone.

CHAPTER 32

THE ANGRY PLACE...

In looking at the stages of grief, I felt I needed to focus more time on one particular stage because I feel it has had the strongest impact on me. It is a stage I fear, a stage whose intensity can shake the strongest foundation and whose power can be relentless if you let it.

Today I can breathe deeply as I say I have moved from this stage. While there are moments still where it tries to suck me back in, I have made progress. I am reminded of one of my favorite Dr. Seuss books, *Oh the Places You'll Go*, how it details a crazed and wild journey of unexpected twists and turns, right up until you find yourself, "Headed, I fear, to a most useless place...The Waiting Place."

For me, this is my parallel universe. I have found myself in my own useless place. I like to call it the Angry Place. In his book, Dr. Seuss's Waiting Place is an unsettling place to be, and no good seems to come of it at all. I feel much the same about the Angry Place.

I fear I could have been there for an eternity, just stewing in my anger. Angry at my OBGYN for not recognizing Sofie's distress during labor, for not removing her from my body after her first cord compression at thirty-five weeks, angry for allowing me to go past my due date, which only seemed to put her further at risk. I am angry at myself for not being able to protect my baby girl, angry at

121

every other pregnant woman who crossed my path simply because she was likely going to have what I was not able to, and of course angry at God for allowing this to happen at all. I do believe I was rescued from this place by my dear husband. He has always adopted the "anger doesn't bring her back" attitude. His strength and support pulled me out of the depths of that place, that awful, dirty, ugly, scary Angry Place.

Letting go of the anger at God, at my OBGYN, and at the universe was relieving. Anger has a disgusting way of clutching on to you and cutting off the supply of peace to your life. Anger twists everything, every moment, and every situation and turns it into something hideous. It doesn't feel good. It feels toxic, like your life is being poisoned.

In the beginning, when I would be out running an errand, I wanted people to feel as badly for me as I did for myself. I was infuriated by every pregnant woman and every woman I saw carrying a car seat filled with a brand-new baby. I was so mad at them—mad that they got what I was supposed to have. I was mad at them, and I didn't even know them. This is not me.

I finally found a way to loosen myself from the vice grips of anger. I would see a pregnant woman and instead of being angry at her, I would cautiously wonder if her baby would make it into the world the way she was expecting, and I would hope that it did. If I couldn't wish for that baby's healthy arrival, what kind of person would that make me? I don't ever want to find out. I would also remind myself that this could be her first pregnancy after losing a child, and then I would find myself rooting for her and that unborn babe.

I would see women carrying around their beautiful, healthy baby girls, and I would remind myself that this baby might not be this woman's only child, that she herself may have walked the very journey of having lost a previous little one and that this may be the first time she is able to care for a living child after a loss.

It is a constant reminder that we truly do not know what it's like to walk in others' shoes. That has helped me to let go of my anger. I can't say there isn't a small piece of me that isn't jealous when I see a new mother showing off her healthy baby. I am jealous that Sofie and I never had those moments. But I would never wish anything different on any pregnant woman because no person should suffer this loss.

I remind myself constantly that while I miss Sofie to depths that I couldn't know existed, I love her even more than I miss her, and that love helps me focus on the joy of celebrating her life instead of losing myself in the anger of her death. Grief is a process. It isn't linear, and there is no ending, at least not in my lifetime.

CHAPTER 33

RESUMING...

As this weekend comes to a close, I am forced to face the reality that with it nears the end of my maternity leave. Twelve weeks that should have been filled with such different days have come and gone. On Monday I return to work. I have so many mixed emotions about this return. I know a routine will be good for me. I know it will be good to see my friends and wonderfully supportive co-workers, but it also means my life must resume now without Sofie, and that is terrifyingly awful.

Sunday night draws to a close. I wait for Mike to fall asleep before I head to bed. He has had to be so strong for me so many times. I don't want to burden him with my weakness tonight.

I find myself doing something I haven't done in a couple of weeks. I simply cry myself to sleep. I feel like that little kid who is so afraid to start at a new school, who cries and sobs until her little body simply tuckers out; that is me. I talk to Sofie. I tell her that I am sorry I won't be spending every single second tomorrow thinking of her, though I suspect that I still will. I ask her to please be ever so close to me, "Because Mama is going to need your help to make it through the day." It's a tall order for such a little girl, and I hate that I'm always reaching out to her for strength and asking her to watch over me when I should be tending to her every need. Once again, this Sunday brings many tears until I drift to sleep.

Monday morning comes so quickly. It doesn't care that I'm not ready; it is here. I tell Mike I'm not ready but that I also know I won't be ready to resume my life six months from now either. I will never be ready to move on without Sofie.

Mike supports me. "You've already faced the worst thing you will ever have to face, so at least today won't be as bad as that."

He is right. In our twisted new perspectives on life, I will never have a worse day than the day we had to say good-bye to our beautiful girl. If I can muster the strength to let my sweet baby go from this world, I can survive going to work.

I get dressed, pack my lunch, and head off toward the hospital, the place where Sofie lived for twenty days. As I walk in, I immediately notice the glass on the bridge has been decoratively painted by our volunteers. The first image I see today is a bright yellow painted butterfly. It makes me smile and feel a little bit stronger for the moment.

I start down the long hallway to my office, and with each step my head is shouting, "This is your life. Like it or not, this is your life!" With each step, my eyes well up more and more. I make it to the door just before my office before the tears flow freely down my cheeks. I am greeted by two colleagues who close the door behind me and just sit in that moment with me, letting me have it for as long as I need. All I can manage is to repeat out loud, "This is weird. This is just so weird."

And it is. I can't even describe it in words because I don't think there are any words in existence to adequately describe the feelings you have after losing a child. I guess I should research the ugliest, meanest, cruelest word that exists in the English language and call it that.

I wipe the tears that are clouding my eyes and joke that to be fair I probably would have cried today even if Sofie had been in day care. My colleagues smile through their own misty eyes and console me. I turn to my desk and notice that my good friend Ted has placed two beautifully framed pictures of me and Sof on my desk along with several small wallet-size prints so I can proudly wear her photo attached to my badge, just like all of the other parents do who work here. It was perfect. To come back and have her beautifully displayed in front of me by someone other than me meant the world and showed such true care of my baby girl.

The day continues, and I feel the support of everyone around me. It still feels weird or that other ugly and disgusting word, whatever that may be. I tell everyone how it is strange to show up to a job I have done for eight years and suddenly feel like a completely different person doing that job now. I look the same but could not be more different.

I feel like my head and heart are continually screaming Sofie's name and reminders of her, which makes it next to impossible to focus on anything else. I imagine it will always be like that, but maybe one day that screaming will be a little quieter, background music, if you will. The kind of background music that sometimes appears so deafening and noticeable, yet other times it becomes a part of your silence. That is OK because I never want it to go away completely, and I know it never will.

I describe my last twelve weeks as a constant dream state. It's one of those dreams that doesn't make any sense but feels too real for comfort. It's like opening your eyes under water. It's fuzzy, groggy, and cloudy, but it continues. I still can't wake up from it.

I tell those closest to me that if they want to have a small understanding of what it feels like, they should stay awake with no sleep at all for at least thirty-six to forty-eight hours, then have a few bottles of beer or glasses of wine, and then just as you try to focus or concentrate on something, have someone stand directly next to you, screaming in your ear. It is fuzzy, distracting, and frustrating, and it is my new normal.

I look at my pager to check the time, and it says that it is 3:48 a.m. on January 1; oh how I wish that were true. For a spilt second I think, *Maybe it worked! Maybe all of my prayers to wake up from this and have it still be January with a healthy, active Sofie safely inside have come true!* But the fuzzy, groggy dream that is my life continues without concern for my broken heart.

I survive the day and know I should feel good about that. Why I deserve any credit for making it through one work day I don't know, but that's what everyone tells me. I don't feel good though. It feels terrible to have my life go on without Sofie here. I feel in some way that I am denying her by being back at work because I cannot focus on her every single second of every day. I feel like if I focus on someone else's needs or offer support to a family that is facing a difficult time that I am somehow denying her. I don't even know if that makes any sense, but it is how it feels. I'm not ready for my life to continue without her. With me being back to work, it makes my hope for that miracle of waking up back in January to Sofie kicking me healthily in the ribs fade with each day. (I know I probably just need to give up on the hope for that miracle altogether, but I think I will hope for that until the day I die.)

Alas, the day has come to a close. I think I did OK. I hate that this is my life, but whoever hands the lives out didn't consult me. They didn't ask me if I wanted it. I didn't sign up for it, but it has been given to me against my will, and I have not yet found a way to trade it in for the life we were supposed to have.

I often say that I am done with 2011. What a sucky, awful year. But it was also filled with such love and hope, and it did bring Sofie into this world, so I can't hate it entirely. I am a better person for having her. I hate, hate, hate that she is not here tonight, that I didn't get to scoop her up from her first day of day care, but as I have said before, I love her...even more than I miss her. Despite all of the pain and sorrow, I am so glad that I had her—that I was given the chance to know and love her, even if it wasn't in the way I had planned.

OK, I think I am done with this grief thing now. I did my very best. Now can I please have my baby girl back?

I just found a container of ice cream in the refrigerator. It makes me love my husband even more right now. It really is nice to know that I'm not alone in this fuzzy-headed world. And Sofie, the smile it brought, that was for you, baby girl.

—*Facebook status update: April 19, 2011*

Chapter 34

Another Day with the New Life...

This day has also found me against my will. All of the hiding under covers, keeping busy with mindless activities, and cowering deep inside of my heart didn't help; here I am. It is my first week back at work, and while I survived yesterday, I have to do it again.

I always imagined my first week back being difficult, but this is nothing like I had planned. I should be frantically getting things ready to ensure I don't forget anything she needs at day care. I should be stressing out over getting myself dressed and ready while trying to get her fed, all while keeping an eye on the time so I won't be late.

I should have butterflies in my stomach because I know it is going to break my heart if she cries when I leave her, but I would give anything to hear those cries now because they would be followed by the joy in her eyes when I would arrive to pick her up. But I don't get to see that joy in her eyes—not today; not ever. The only thing that has remained unchanged from my expectations of this day is how sad I am to be away from my baby girl, only this sadness doesn't go away with the end of my workday.

The feeling that I am starting out an entirely new job for which I am inadequately prepared seems to have grown overnight. I am looking through the world with a new set of eyes, and I'm still adjusting to the light. Everything looks different. Everything is different. I know I still look like me, but I don't feel like me, at least not the old me. And I'm not used to this new me just yet.

I enter the hospital, and even today it feels so different. You know how it feels when you find the perfect pair of shoes? You know the ones you have been searching for everywhere, only they are one size too small? But there are no others you like and these are perfect. So you buy them anyway, knowing that in time maybe you can get them to stretch a bit…and besides, isn't it always fashion over function?

You put on the new shoes and they are snug, too tight against your poor feet. Instantly your feet begin to throb in protest, almost becoming numb as they adjust to this awkward fit. With each step they rub against the back of your ankles, leaving them more raw and sensitive with every stride. You can barely stretch your feet while you walk because of the twinging discomfort; but they *do* look good, like a new pair of shoes should.

Everyone compliments you on your new shoes and how good they look. They don't know the pain you are enduring with each step. Some moments the pain grows so severe that you have to sit down for a minute. Other times your feet get used to the pain and numbness. You barely notice how they tightly hug your feet until the next time the pain sharpens and catches you off guard.

My life now feels like these shoes that are one size too small (though some days it feels like they are ten sizes too small). People compliment my strength and how good it is to see me. They have no idea of the constant pain and discomfort that I am reminded of with each step throughout my new life. Sure, you can focus on other things while you walk in these new shoes, but you are always aware of them, just hoping for them to stretch out and feel a little more comfortable. I'm still waiting for that part; I imagine I'll be waiting for a long, long time.

I wonder if I'll have the gift of focus once again. Things that I could do with ease just months before now seem to take every flickering brain cell. The most mundane tasks require my mind to fight the battle of the background music.

The moment I open my eyes in the morning, its chorus in my head begins: Sofie, Sofie, Sofie. I wish she were here. It's not January; this really *has* happened. Good morning, sweet pea. I miss you. Sofie! Sofie! Sofie! Grab some breakfast. God, I wish I were feeding her. (Tears.) Sofie, Sofie. I should wash laundry. (Heart aches.) I wish I were washing dozens of loads of her little clothes instead. Sofie, Sofie, why am I in my bedroom? I think I'll go read her a book. I should be holding her while I read to her. (Many tears.) Sofie, Sofie…I'll go get the mail. I am so tired; maybe a short rest. (Restless napping.) Sofie, Sofie….I better start dinner. Why is the mail in the refrigerator? Sofie, Sofie. It's the end of the day. I yearn to bathe her and get her ready for bed. (More tears.) Mike is home. I am trying to listen to him talk, but I can't focus. I just want Sofie. I miss her. Why can't we just go back and have her be fine? Why her? Sofie, Sofie…it's time for bed. Why do I not have any clean clothes for tomorrow? Sofie, Sofie… (Eyes close; drift to sleep. Wake tomorrow and repeat.)

Grief is exhausting. I ease into the workday today, which is helpful. Somebody I'm talking with sees a picture of Sof on my badge and asks, "Who is this beautiful baby?"

I reply proudly, "She is my daughter."

"What is her name?"

I smile and say, "Sofia." One test passed. It feels good.

Many co-workers find me throughout the day; one in particular seeks me out. Tearfully and angrily she asks, "I just don't understand what happened?"

She is passionate; there is no doubting her concern or feeling of injustice. But reliving every awful moment of the tragic parts and not focusing on the beautiful part—on Sofie herself—is hard for me. I have been doing so much better focusing on the moments that I did have with her, how much she inspires me, and my love for her. I haven't felt angry in many days. But this person is angry for me, she cares so much.

"Why didn't your doctor take her out sooner? Why were they OK with her going past her due date? Why?!"

It is frighteningly amazing at how quickly I join her in that anger. Immediately I feel my blood boiling. I am pissed! My doctors should have taken her out before her due date! She would have been fine! They took my daughter away from me!

The rage feels awful. Regardless, this is my situation. Being angry doesn't bring my daughter back. This fierce anger feels like a drug; it is easy and powerful, but it is dangerous. I'm aware of how unhealthy it makes me feel.

I try to breathe, try to swim out of this tidal wave of anger...if I can just stay afloat.

I walk away to clear my head of this poisonous feeling. I see a familiar face down the long hallway. His name is Tim; he has worked here many more years than I. He was one of the first people I ever met when I accepted my job here. Being new at a job is always difficult. You're unsure of yourself, how you'll fit in; who will befriend you, and who will make you feel as if you're just in the way? Tim was extraordinarily kind to me from day one. Our paths at work rarely crossed, but on occasion when they did, it was always refreshing and pleasant.

Today I see him heading my way. I'm immediately faced with this new "oh shit" factor that comes along with my grief. I don't know if he knows. He walks up to me calmly, kisses me on the cheek, and hugs me gently. I see tears in his eyes. He knows. He walks away, never uttering a word.

"Is that all?" I asked quietly, surprised by our simple interaction.

He smiles and nods yes.

I question him further, "Is that the only reason you came all the way up to this unit?" I'm still confused that he sought me out for a hug, but I'm appreciative.

He slowly walks back to me, the tears more noticeable in his eyes now. He comes close and whispers, "It happened to me too, about thirty years ago."

We have a beautiful interaction about his daughter. I am mystified. Eight years and I never knew. I am touched by his tears. I find this moment both comforting and terrifying. It is comforting to know that in thirty years, my love for Sofie will continue to be so strong that it will still bring tears to my eyes, and at the same time, I'm terrified to know that thirty years from now the pain of losing her will still feel so strong that it will bring tears to my eyes as well. But I think I already knew that, and to be completely honest, I wouldn't have it any other way.

I continue to go about my day. A nurse says to me, "I don't know how you come back here after this has happened."

I smile as I explain, "This place is the only place where the three of us were a family, other than for fourteen hours at home. Everyone here knew Sofie, knew of Sofie, and knew us as a family. Even some of our closest friends and family didn't get to witness the three of us as a family doing normal family things. That makes this place comforting. Sofie's existence isn't only known here; she is celebrated and loved. That makes it easier to walk in these doors."

As I end my day, I decide to see one more family. The patient is sleeping, so I speak with her father. He is a wonderful man, one of those people who leaves you feeling better when you walk away. He is interesting and funny and exudes a zest for life. He also happens to be fighting an incredibly aggressive terminal illness. His prognosis is very grim. Yet he smiles. He jokes. He loves. I am thoroughly enjoying listening to him and getting to know more about him and his family. Consistent with his kindness, he shares that he is bringing in brownies for the staff tomorrow and wants to be sure I get one. I jokingly say that I am not working tomorrow but state that I know the staff will appreciate his generosity.

"Not here tomorrow?" he asks.

I proceed with caution as I explain, "I am just here Monday through Wednesday."

"Do you do anything else?"

I feel myself getting anxious. It's hard to explain, but you just know when someone is going to ask. You can feel it from miles away. But I feel prepared—well, as prepared as I can be. I have been practicing a script in my head for very moments like these, and I did pass today's earlier test when somebody asked about my picture of Sofie. I can do this.

I simply reply with a quick, "Nope."

He continues, "Got kids?"

I have promised Sofie that I will never deny her. I will always recognize her as my daughter and will always be proud to do so.

"Yes," I answer. "I have a daughter."

I try to desperately to reroute the conversation back to his daughter. It doesn't work.

"How old?" he asks.

"She would be three months next week," I reply.

He doesn't seem to pick up on the "would be" part. But so far my script is working; there is no flood of tears.

"That wasn't that long ago," he says, surprised.

I explain that this is actually my first week back and again attempt to divert the conversation back to his daughter's admission.

Then it happened; he clearly didn't get a copy of my script. It had been going so well. I had stuck to it, and I felt proud.

But then he adlibbed, "Everyone healthy and happy?"

Who asks that? I mean seriously, in all of my experience around friends and family members who have children, when people ask if they do, they occasionally ask their ages, maybe even their names, but I have never heard anyone get asked if they are all healthy and happy. Couldn't he have just assumed everyone was healthy and happy? Couldn't he have just stuck to the script that I thought had been prepared flawlessly?

The improvisation of the script threw me. I looked at him after what felt like the longest pregnant pause and simply said, "Actually, no, but thank you for asking."

His eyes didn't break contact; he stared intently at me for what seemed like hours. I added, "She actually passed away."

At the same time he started to say he was sorry, I began talking over the "I'm sorrys," hoping I could erase them with my words as I said to him, "It's OK." (Well, it's not OK that she passed away, but it was OK that he asked.)

I continued, "Thank you for giving me the opportunity to acknowledge my daughter."

He then looked at me tenderly and asked softly, "Can I know her name?"

"Sofia," I said proudly.

"It's beautiful," he said. I agreed and once again redirected the conversation back to his little girl.

I never did tear up—well, not until I got back to my office anyway. I was able to have a proud mother moment, acknowledging lovingly that I am her mom.

I hate to think that this wonderful man feels bad for bringing the topic up. This is such a strange phenomenon in grief. People immediately feel terrible for bringing up such a difficult topic, like they have reminded me that Sofie died or have forced me to think about it. They didn't remind me. Believe me, I am incredibly aware of the fact that she is not here 1,440 minutes a day.

I'm struck by a quote that I recalled hearing in the past when Elizabeth Edwards was speaking about the death of her son.

She said, "If you know someone who has lost a child or lost anybody who's important to them and you're afraid to mention them because you think you might make them sad by reminding them that they died, they didn't forget they died. You're not reminding them. What you're reminding them of is that you remember that they lived, and that's a great, great gift."

What this gentle man did for me today was allow me to acknowledge Sofie and to acknowledge myself as her mother. It's something that doesn't often come up anymore since those dark days when I would get to announce it as I spoke into the NICU intercom system in response to the secretary's, "How can I help you?"

"It's Sofia Dente's mom."

"Please come in."

I loved being able to identify myself that way. I hate that I often don't get to anymore. But today I got that. This man gave me that opportunity, that gift. I was able to maintain focus on the good part, the fact that Sofia is my daughter and I am her mother. I was able to acknowledge her, perfectly amazing, just the way she is.

I look back at that exchange often, touched by the joy that exuded from this gentleman as he faced his terminal illness, and I hope people will someday notice that about me as well. I hope I can exude joy, hope, and love to others even as I share the difficult parts of losing Sofie. I hope the joy, hope, and love we have for Sofie can be our proclamation, the part that people notice first rather than the sadness of losing her.

I drive home thankful that my first week back is behind me. The rain is pouring down as I arrive at a stoplight. I wish I was turning right, toward Sofie's day care, where I can scoop her up and revel in the fact that I have her for the next four days at home; instead I stay straight when the light turns green to bring a rose to her grave. I so wish I was turning right; and let the background music continue... "Sofie, Sofie, Sofie, Sofie, Sofie."

CHAPTER 35

A LITTLE SIGN OF SOFIE...

Today I find myself in a place of peace. Today my words aren't a result of sadness, loss, pain, or grief but are filled with a peaceful light. I understand that my feelings of peace today can be ripped away from me with any breath I take or with the next blink of my eye, so for right now, in this very moment, I am clutching this peace close to my heart because it may not be mine to keep.

It is difficult in this new grief state that has come to be my life, to recognize any blessings. I have always been someone who tries to see the good in things, so not being able to wear those rose-colored glasses anymore leaves me that much more feeling like someone else.

But today there is a little glimmer of rose color (or maybe it is a perfect shade of baby pink). As I have spoken with so many parents who have lost their own little ones, I have recognized a blessing I have had. I listen to a number of parents whose children have gone before them discuss how they have never dreamed of their babies. My heartache grew for them as they continued to share that they have never felt their little ones close by.

I recognize that to some people, some things I have said, thought, and believed could come across as far-fetched. I understand that to an innocent bystander, things that come out of my mouth could very well elicit a, "Wow, she seemed so normal until she said that!" type of response. But when I am able to find peace and hope within anything these days, I am going to hold on like heck to that.

I often find myself gently trying to teach people to never judge a grieving mother. I would do anything to connect with my baby girl, to have any reassurance that she is well and at peace—that she is not in pain, not afraid, that somehow she lives on. For those reading who have experienced a similar loss, I don't feel the need to explain this desperation to you because I know you understand. For those of you who have not experienced such a loss, take a moment to give thanks for that, to give thanks for the inability to understand such a desperate need. Just trust me when I tell you that you would do anything to be able to have a connection with your lost child.

I am fully aware that there will be judgment and naysayers as I continue—people who will so willingly offer explanations or coincidence to explain certain things. I can't deny my experiences because they have brought me a peace I have never felt before. I have been painfully open through my experience, so I do believe this peace should be shared as well.

I continue to connect and communicate with Sofie daily. I know I'm not alone in this; I know many people who have lost loved ones will ask for and look for signs to give them any reassurance that their loved one is OK. I began reading books about these after-death communications and felt that much more validated in what I have experienced with my own sweet girl.

Today I am thankful for some amazing connections I have experienced with Sof. I have had the incredible gift of seeing her in my dreams, in dreams where I felt I was truly blessed by her presence. I have had countless experiences that have granted me signs—very specific signs—that my baby girl lives on. Sure, someone could say that they are all coincidence, but my heart tells me, even in moments when I scrutinize them myself with a strong dose of realism, that they are so much more.

I can't explain or understand why everyone who has lost someone doesn't get to experience this gift of presence or reassurance. I have often told Sof that if I could just meet her every night in my dreams, then perhaps I could manage the loss of her a little bit better. I have not been granted that, I wish I had. I wish everyone who is grieving could recognize and know that their loved ones are still very much a part of their everyday lives.

I have experienced things that I don't believe can be explained or chalked up as coincidence. I look forward to experiencing more of these. They are little glimpses of my baby girl's heavenly life, and they bring such an intense joy and a peace like no other.

That doesn't mean I don't still miss her every minute of every day to the point where I cry unrelenting tears. That doesn't mean I wouldn't give anything to have her back with me the way I had planned. That doesn't mean I still don't go to bed every night wishing it will be January when I wake up so we can alter this ending. But it does mean that every day, I feel her. It does mean that she is a real part of my every day, and today, that means everything.

I have reserved a lot of my signs, stories, and dreams just for myself, Mike, and some close family and friends. Those experiences are too sacred to me to share with the world, and I don't feel they are meant to be. I hope you can understand.

What I will leave you with is a request for you to open yourselves to the things around you every day. Breathe deeply, trust your instincts, and quiet yourself. Open your hearts and your minds, and with that openness may you be blessed with some extraordinary experiences.

I will leave you with a little sign of Sofie that occurred early in the morning that felt significant.

This morning while I was talking to Mike on the phone, I was standing in front of our sliding glass door, looking out into the gray, snowy day. I was taken aback by a small bird that was seemingly out of place as it sat on our deck in the middle of a snowstorm. It looked happily content as it gazed in my direction. The bird didn't seem to falter as I made noise or movement toward it; it just stayed there. I told Mike about our little visitor, and he said that he too had noticed a lot of birds this morning by Sofie's grave. I remind him that in one of our favorite books we read to her, there is a line that says if, "a little bird sits at your window awhile, it's because it's hoping to see you smile." I tell Mike that I wonder if Sofie wants to see us smile today.

After we hang up, I head to her nursery and decide to read her that book, *On the Night You Were Born*, by Nancy Tillman. I climb into the glider, wishing she were in my arms, and begin.

There are many lines from this book that have become favorites of mine. It was a challenge in the hospital to read Sofie books that felt appropriate given our unique situation. This one was a gift to us that I treasure.

One of my favorite lines reads, "So whenever you doubt just how special you are and you wonder who loves you, how much and how far, listen for the geese honking high in the sky. (They're singing a song to remember you by.)" This part always makes me tear up when I read it to Sof.

After I finish the book, I laugh as I say to her out loud, "Well, sweet pea, we certainly don't hear a lot of geese around here, so I'll just take that little bird on the deck as my sign for the day. I love you, baby girl."

I leave her nursery and get ready to start my day. When I walk outside, I am stopped in my tracks; all I can hear is geese honking overhead. I never see them, but I hear them, loud as can be, singing their song to remember her by.

CHAPTER 36

THE GIRL WITH THE PINK CONVERSE SHOES...

Right side of the center aisle, seventeen rows back. Week after week since Sofie has died, I find myself back in this pew. I have kept my promise to Sofie. I continue to come to church with her daddy, and I use this hour to sit in her presence.

Early in my pregnancy, I would often notice a family that was also a regular at this service, a family of four; mom, dad, sister, and little brother. The little girl, no more than six years old, is always the picture of style. Casual chic, if you will, and was always adorning the most adorable pink Converse shoes. I remember, thinking back, how I couldn't wait to see Sofie one day wearing the same pink Converse shoes that say, "I'm fashionable, adorable, sassy, and cool."

I haven't thought of this little girl since everything has happened. Tonight these pink Converse shoes shake me to my core. I will never see Sofie in them. I will never even have Sofie by my side in this church. No baptism here, no first communion, no confirmation, no wedding. No pink Converse shoes for her.

Every week I walk into church and am filled with a myriad of emotions. This place, this exquisite building, once captured such a joy-filled day of hope and love as I walked down the long aisle to stand by her daddy and unite as one. That same aisle seemed so cold and terrifying the morning of her funeral.

I find myself in a different place each week. Sure, we still sit in row seventeen on the right side of the center aisle, but every week I am becoming someone new. I mourn that we don't get to carry in our car seat with our beautiful baby girl inside. I mourn that I don't have a reason to sit with her in the crying room, to bring in her toys and hope we can distract her enough for the hour to not disrupt those around us. I mourn the loss of people "peacing" Sofie when she was growing inside of me every week. I mourn these small yet monumental things week after week.

But I don't hate being in this church anymore either. My anger has been fading. I can't say there aren't moments when I don't still question what *He* was thinking. There are plenty of moments when I still sob for what should have been. But the anger I have felt was toxic. I never want to think of my baby girl and feel that way. I only want to think of her and feel pure love.

I have sat in this church heartbroken, angry, and like a stubborn teenager, trying with all my might to ignore God and His prayers; after all, I felt that He ignored me and mine.

But that relationship is healing. A dear doctor in the hospital told me one day, "It's OK to be mad at God because that means you are at least still in a relationship with Him. It is when you feel indifferent that there is a problem."

She was right. Many times I wanted to be indifferent. But I would find myself yelling at God, screaming at how much I didn't care about Him, how much I hated Him. But I continued screaming. Why would I scream and yell at someone if I really didn't care? If I tried to give Him the silent treatment and not talk to or scream at Him at all, I couldn't deny that I would continue to think about Him throughout the day.

In conversations with my sister in law, Cathy, who also lost a child, we would both share how it is so disheartening when you feel that not only will God not answer your prayers but neither will the forces of evil. There were so many hours during our hospital stay where I would have given up everything for Sofie's survival, I mean everything— peaceful eternity for a lifetime in hell if it would save my baby girl.

But not only did I feel a great silence from God, there was no evil presence taking me up on my offer either. And that silence was deafening, shaking any ounce of faith I had inside of me.

On my darkest of days, I questioned, "Where is God?" I now understand that He was everywhere. I believe that God cared so much about me that He wouldn't allow me to make such a deal with evil. I believe God was raising me up, giving me the strength I would need to make the very best decisions for my baby girl.

Some people will say, "Everything happens for a reason." I tend to roll my eyes. What reason could ever be good enough for taking any baby, for taking Sofie? People will say, "God has a plan," to which I think, *Well if He does, it is a stupid, stupid plan!*

Father Kraker said tonight, "God knows and does what is best for us, and we need to trust that."

My first thought was, *Really? How is this best for us?* Then I took a moment to look outside of my own self for a minute and realized that there is truth to this statement. Perhaps it wasn't about me at all. That was a shocking thought in my complete state of selfishness.

Sofie compressed her umbilical cord, and she had severe brain damage. Perhaps God used Mike and me to make the decisions we did because it was the best for her. Perhaps God couldn't stop her from compressing her cord. Perhaps He couldn't restore her to health the way I and so many others had hoped and prayed. Perhaps He cried for her life being cut so short as well. But allowing her to die peacefully, to leave this world that had been much too difficult and cruel to her, perhaps that was the best thing for her in her injured state. And in our devastated state, I now believe God did what was best for us as well. He allowed us the ability to focus all of our difficult decisions on solely what we believed was best for Sofie. He alone is the only explanation I can provide for having the strength to let our sweet girl go.

I do not believe God gave me Sofie just to have it end like it did. I don't believe He created her to take her away just as we were about to meet her. I do not and *cannot* believe that God's plan was for this to happen to Sofie. I don't believe He caused her to compress her cord.

I do believe He created her perfectly to be the beautiful little girl He intended, but the cord accident got in the way. I do believe that in spite of that tragedy, He allowed her to be the inspiration of love in just twenty-one short days that she would have inspired throughout her life time.

Father Kraker went on to speak about parental love, something I certainly understand. He told a story: "There was woman who strayed from her relationship with God. As her life was drawing to an end, the distance she created between herself and God began to concern her. A clergymen who went to visit her noticed beautiful photos atop her mantle, displayed with such pride. He asked about the people in the photos. They were her children and grandchildren, she explained, beaming with joy. The clergyman asked if any of them had ever done anything over the years to disappoint her—maybe not called when they said they would, maybe even gone a period of time without speaking or not visiting when she had hoped they would. She nodded her head with an 'of course' attitude. He continued to ask if there was anything they could have done that would have caused her to take their photo off of that mantle. Without a second thought, she exclaimed, 'No!' He looked at her tenderly and explained that God beams with that same joy when thinking of her."

God and I have had many conversations, some nicer than others. We are healing. He knows how much I love Sofie, so I believe He understands. I sit in church more willingly these days. I listen to the readings, and I participate in the prayers. Mike and I even brought the gifts up during the service tonight. I have yet to make it through an entire mass without tears filling my eyes at some point. Maybe I'll get there; maybe I won't. I now feel that God is holding me closely during those moments, weeping with me.

Every week after mass has ended, Mike and I light a candle for Sofie. Every week I wish that she had been there with us, the way we had planned. But every week, I make time to sit in this beautiful church and remember my baby girl.

When I think of what Sofie is doing in heaven in those moments when we are at church, I wonder if she is sitting in God's lap. I picture her with her tiny little hands cupping the very face of God, nuzzling Him and His beard, just loving Him. I know we've all been taught that God loves everyone equally, but my hunch is that even He has a special place in His heart for Sof.

God, thank You for blessing me with the gift of Sofia. While she was only in my arms for twenty-one short days, she is in my heart forever. Thank you for choosing me to be her mother. I'm sorry for my moments of doubt and those moments of sheer anger. I ask for forgiveness and ask that you continue to give me strength to focus on the love I have for her. Help me to continue to be the best mama to her that I can be.

God, please take care of my baby girl until I get there. Please keep her in Your peace and light. I read somewhere along my grief journey, "They say that time in heaven is compared to 'the blink of an eye' for us on this earth. Sometimes it helps me to think of my child running ahead of me through a beautiful field of wildflowers and butterflies; so happy and completely caught up in what she is doing that when she looks behind her, I'll already be there."

I do hope that is how it will be for Sof. May she be joy-filled and carefree every moment until I can be there to rock her in my arms once again. May she be the first to greet me as I walk my own journey into heaven one day. May she lead me gently toward Your grace and light, and maybe, just maybe, she'll be wearing those pink Converse shoes.

CHAPTER 37

LIFE LESSON NUMBER 2,349 FROM A BABY GIRL TO HER MAMA...

Today I am heading to my annual dermatology appointment; no, not for Botox (though my eyes could definitely use some!), just for an annual preventative skin check. I love this doctor's office. It is incredibly posh and way overindulgent. Typically when coming here, I make sure I am in a cute, trendy outfit, with my hair and makeup well done, and looking my best. A bit vain, yes, but after all, these people evaluate people's outer self for a living.

Today, however, is different. I have that first day of school pit in my stomach feeling as I get ready. Today I find myself in this beautifully decorated, posh waiting room wearing shorts, a ragged, plain T-shirt with my hair up and no makeup at all. The poor girl behind the desk is probably thinking, *Whoa! Whatever she is getting done, they sure have their work cut out for them!*

Today's appointment feels daunting. You see, this is the last of appointments (believe me, there were many) where the last time I was here I let them know I was pregnant. My doctor was so excited that not only did she document it in my chart, but she also scrolled it across the top bar of the computer screen. Now today, when that computer screen pops up, they will ask about the baby. My heart is heavy.

My name is called, and I am escorted to the exam room. The nurse tech checking me in is very kind. I cringe as she pulls up the computer screen. I wonder after this visit if it will scroll "dead baby" across the top.

She says nothing. She asks me all of the routine questions: "How much time do you spend in the sun? Do you still live at…? Any medicine changes? Any recent surgeries or procedures we need to know about?" My heart gets caught in my throat; I gave birth…my baby died. But I don't think that is what she means, so I reply with a no.

That is it. She is done with her part. Phew. I feel like I dodged a bullet to the heart. Well to be honest, a bullet to the heart would be a blessing. It would be fast and basically painless, and it wouldn't cause agonizing suffering.

Before the tech leaves the room, she spots my necklace, the one on which I had Sofie's handprints and footprints engraved. She comes closer to see it and asks, "Is that your baby's prints?" I respond proudly back with a yes.

I love my necklace with her tiny prints, but I can't tell you how few people acknowledge them (except those who knew I was having them made). This was a welcome interaction.

I sit in the exam room for forty-five minutes, freezing because the paper dress they have me wearing is no match for the room's arctic chill. I flash back to my last appointment. I was eight weeks pregnant. I was so excited to tell my doctor. She kept telling me how I was "just beaming," and having known of our earlier miscarriage, she kept assuring me that she "just knew this pregnancy was going to be alright." (That's something I will never say to any pregnant woman because unfortunately no one can ever guarantee that).

My heart hasn't yet found its way out of my throat, and I feel my eyes beginning to well up. *Please don't cry—not yet, not here.* This is the last time I have to tell someone who is expecting a joy-filled story about the heartache that has accompanied it (though my heart and my head know this won't be the last time).

I compose myself minutes before my doctor and the nurse come in. As they position me on the exam table, the nurse immediately asks me if my bracelet is a "mother's bracelet." It is my silver and garnet bracelet that spells Sofie's beautiful name, again one that has gone seemingly unnoticed even though I have worn it every day. I nervously tell her yes.

She comments, "It is beautiful. I have one as well and wear it all the time." I feel like a normal mom.

The doctor didn't look at the computer screen and doesn't seem to remember my joyous announcement from my last visit; I am more than fine with this. She flips me over onto my back, and as she examines my stomach, she notices my linea nigra.

She asks, "Have you been pregnant recently?"

I gulp back my heart and tell her, "I had a baby in January."

"What day?"

"The twenty-sixth," I reply.

She smiles. She notices my necklaces and reads Sofia Isabella's name out loud. "Is this is your first?"

"Yes."

She smiles. "I have one that was born in January too. Sofia is going to be incredibly independent."

If only she knew just how independent. She doesn't need her mama at all. There is so little that I can even do for her.

The exam is over. I have made it through with no tears—not in the office anyway. I get to the car, and it is a different story. The tears flow freely as my mind processes the morning.

In the background a familiar song comes on the radio that I have heard countless times, but my understanding of the words are so different now. It is "Bad Day" by Daniel Powter.

Isn't that the truth? I am having a low moment in the car; my baby is so independent she doesn't even need me at all. This is a difficult pill to swallow. As I cross an upcoming street, I notice its blurry name through my tear-filled eyes: Legacy Drive.

I replay this morning's events. I dreaded having to share with another person who expected a happy story that my beautiful baby had died. Today I didn't have to.

I was able to share Sofie. I shared her beautiful little prints, her lovely name, and her birthday…only. I only shared that she lived, the part the matters the most. Her life is her legacy, not her death. She began inspiring love, hope, and faith at the moment she entered this life, not because she left it. I begin to feel joy win out over the pain at my revelation. Sofie's life is her legacy! Just as I ask her out loud, "You aren't done yet, are you, baby girl?" a beautiful, large yellow and black butterfly flies right across my windshield. Coincidence? Perhaps. Special? Definitely!

She isn't done yet; she's got so much more to share. My baby girl may be independent, but just maybe she does need me. She needs me to continue her legacy, to continue to share her life so she can continue to spread her love.

I promise you, baby girl, your mama's not done yet either. I will always share your story but more importantly your life so you can continue to awaken a sense of love in every heart that learns of you. I love you, sweet pea.

CHAPTER 38

LOVE.

Today is a crisp January morning. The sunlight shimmers off of the morning dew. It is a gentle and serene start to the day. With a steaming cup of coffee in hand, I am compelled to begin my day by writing a letter to my dear girl. I nestle into a comfy corner on the couch with her puppy dogs close by and begin.

Sofie,

For the past few weeks, I had the honor of being able to share you, your life, and our story with the folks your mama works with every day. It was an intimate look into how our lives have changed since you entered the world.

As I sit down to write this, I am immediately struck by one of the cards you received in the hospital that I just re-read the other day. It begins, "Dear Sofie, you were born to change the people around you forever, first your parents and then everyone else. You have already made people look to God more than ever. Great start."

I choke up every time I read those words, not just out of sadness because I miss you terribly but out of the sheer power of those statements.

You were born to change the people around you forever, and that you did. Great start.

When I look back toward the early days of our journey, I feel like I lost myself in the obvious lessons. You know, the "life is unfair and terribly unbalanced" lesson. Sometimes it was hard for me to see through the cloud of tears in my eyes to recognize fully the most powerful lessons you have taught not only me but also so many who have been touched by you: the lesson of love.

For twelve months, when people have asked me how I let go of my anger and continue to face each day, my answer has never changed. "I miss her terribly, every second of every day but I love her even more than I miss her." I choose to focus on that love even in those dark, difficult moments…I learned that from your daddy.

When people have asked me how I feel like I have changed over this time, my answer is simple: "She has taught me how to live and love differently." Love is everywhere to be found when I think of you, sweet baby girl. Love gives me joy, strength, faith, and hope. You are love.

I was recently asked to share our story at an annual work retreat for all of the nurses and doctors in the intensive care unit where I work. It was a beautiful opportunity to reconnect staff with each other but mostly with their purpose for doing what they do every day. I was honored to be a part of the experience in this way. For a full day, we holed away in a cabin in the woods where we learned, laughed, and cried together.

As I was preparing to share my perspectives as a grieving parent with the last batch of my co-workers, I reflected on many things from the past few weeks: A difficult Thanksgiving holiday in which you should have been slinging sweet potatoes at your daddy and me, but instead there was not a single food stain on our clothes from you. I breathed deeply as we were hurled into the next holiday season with reminders of just how special, amazing, and different this Christmas was supposed to be as we experienced the joy of Christmas through the eyes of our eleven-month-old baby girl. Instead we celebrated you at an annual remembrance service for children who have left us much too soon.

I reflected back to the first session of our work retreat and was overcome as I kept playing and replaying some very wise words that were shared that day.

"Every sentence has a period." Our lives on this earth are final. "Every sentence has a period." Those words struck me the minute they were spoken. My initial reaction was to respond with, "I don't want a period at the end of my sentence. I want an exclamation point!" But as the week went on and I thought about you, your daddy, and our beautiful family of three, you changed my perspective once again.

Every sentence does have a period. It doesn't matter what kind of car you drive, how much money you make, or how successful you are, that period will find its way to the end of your sentence. It doesn't matter how much crying, pleading, praying, yelling, kicking, or screaming we do (trust me, I know), we cannot escape that period. But it isn't the period that matters; it is the words of your sentence that make a statement (pun intended).

Think about it—every sentence that is read, be it clever, funny, sad, thrilling, short, long, run-on, grammatically correct or not; every sentence is read the same. The period is never spoken. It is assumed. It is there. We see it, we acknowledge and regard it, but it is not mentioned. What is mentioned—the parts that evoke emotions of love, fear, anxiety, thrill, joy, or hope or invite laughter—are the words of that sentence. The period is not what matters.

The words of our life sentence is what matters the most. We never know when that period is coming, so we need to make sure our sentence is complete and makes the statement we want to make. Some sentences are very long, and others are average length. Your sentence was much too short for your daddy and me. I do wish it had gone on for chapters and chapters. (But my heart knows it still does.)

When I was sharing our story and our lives together, my head kept inquiring, "What is Sofie's sentence?" I kept envisioning your short sentence over and over again, and it never changed. Love. Period. And that, sweet baby girl, is one pretty powerful statement.

I'm not sure my sentence is complete, but it is much more the statement that I want it to be today because of you. As long as my sentence has you in it, then I know it will be a statement I can be proud of.

When it is time for that period to find its way to me, I hope that the Great Writer places your sentence just before and just after mine. Love. You encompass my statement; your life and our love, together with your daddy's…those are some sentences I think are worth reading. Love.

"So faith, hope, love remain, these three; but the greatest of these is love" (1 Cor. 13:13).

It is better to light a single candle, than to curse the darkness.

—Chinese Proverb

Chapter 39

Dancing Through...

I feel like I have been on this journey forever, and in other ways it feels as if it is just beginning. In some ways I feel like just yesterday I was preparing for my life to be so different, so full of dreams of what was supposed to be. Other days it feels like the last time I felt Sofie kick inside of me was a lifetime ago. I guess it was. It was the end of my first life. You see, I am unique; I have lived two lives.

My life as I knew it and had prepared for ended the night Sofie was born, and my new life began. I can't explain in words what it feels like to have lived two lives in one lifetime. Those who have been there, I know that you get it, and I hate that you do. Please accept my deepest sorrow and accept my love and hope for you pouring through my words.

Those of you who cannot understand the feeling, thank God for that! I wouldn't want anyone to ever have to feel the painful void of losing a child. No one should ever be able to even imagine this, let alone live it.

As difficult as this journey has been, I can't look back on this complete experience and wish that it never happened. I can't disregard this entire year as a giant slap in the face or kick to the heart because Sofie was a part of it. Sure, it wasn't at all as I had hoped, dreamed, or planned, but Sofie *was* brought into our lives.

It is difficult to explain how I can now look back at her birthday with feelings of such joy and heartache all rolled into one. To feel the two most extreme feelings that I have ever felt and to have felt them completely tangled and intertwined is impossible to describe.

It was the most terrifyingly devastating yet happiest moment of my life. I know it makes no sense, but welcome to the world of losing your baby. None of it makes sense, just like the fact that there is no title to describe a bereaved parent. If you lose your spouse, you become a widow or widower. If your parents are deceased, you are known as an orphan. However, there is no word to describe what a parent becomes after losing a child, and that is a perfect example of just how ridiculous and unnatural the whole experience is. There isn't even a word for it in the English language. It just shouldn't be.

Many people would tell me in the days right after Sofie's passing, "I don't know how you do it. I don't know how you face each day." The way I see it, I can either drown in these awful feelings of grief, wallowing in my completely broken heart, or I can just try to survive. I have opted for the latter.

Sofie had to endure difficulties that a newborn baby girl should never have to. I will now live my life because she never got the chance to live hers. I choose not to waste my life despite my sadness because that does not honor her in any way. If I stay in bed crying all day, unshowered, refusing to leave the house, that does not honor the inspiration and love she brought to me and to so many others. I will do everything in honor of her.

On some days I get out of bed only for her. I get showered and dressed just for her. I leave the house daily because of her. I breathe for her. I will spend every day finding ways to honor her. She gives my life purpose, and now I live my life for her. I am her mother, and I will find ways every day to continue to parent her. She is the only child Mike

156

and I have. Parenting an angel is the only kind of parenting we know, and I will proudly be her mother every day.

That doesn't mean there aren't moments, days even, when I want to give up, when I find myself sobbing uncontrollably, clutching a pair of her pajamas that I thank God still somehow smell like her. I still have days when I wake up and think, *Well at least today I am one day closer to the end of my life and seeing her again.* I do have those moments, those days. But then I am reminded that I am no longer living my life for me. I am solely waking up every day and living for her, and that gives me purpose and drive.

I have said it before, but I can't stress it enough. I miss her desperately, every second of every day, *but* I love her more than I miss her. That love helps me face each day.

Life is messy. It is not at all what I had expected. I have felt blessed and cursed all in the same moment. But it is my life. Sofie is my daughter, and I would take all of the pain and hurt of losing her all over again if it means getting the chance to have had her at all.

Sometimes I joke with Sofie when I look back at our pregnancy. I recall how careful I was twenty-four hours a day trying to ensure her safety in the womb. I often say to myself in the sweet voice that I give her, "Mama, you worried about all the wrong things." But the truth is, had I known where we would be today, I would have loved her no less while she was growing inside of me. I would have done all of the exact same things to give her the best chance possible at growing healthily while I carried her. I would still have declined even a sip of wine on my Italian vacation, still would have overcooked any meat or fish I put into my mouth. I still would have made sure to never miss a prenatal appointment or single vitamin. I would have still decorated her nursery just as beautifully for her, even if I knew she would only spend fourteen hours inside of it. It is what she deserved, and I have no regrets about that.

Life isn't always good, and it most certainly isn't always fair, but it is life. It is ours, and it is the only one that we get. The only certainty in life is the uncertainty of life. I am a walking example that in just one day, in just one breath, in just one push, your life can be changed forever.

You've heard it said many times, "Live every day as if it is your last." I challenge you instead to live every day as if it is the last day of the people around you because then we will meet each other with more kindness, forgiveness, compassion, and love.

I had nine amazing months of falling in absolute love with my baby girl, and then I had twenty-one days with her in my arms. She has changed my entire world. Her handprint is on my heart and my heart is that much better because of her.

An old friend shared this with me in the days after losing Sofie:

> You will lose someone you can't live without, and your heart will be badly broken, and the bad news is that you never completely get over the loss of your beloved. But this is also the good news. They live forever in your broken heart that doesn't seal back up. It's like having a broken leg that never heals perfectly—that still hurts when the weather gets cold, but you learn to dance with the limp.
>
> —Anne Lamott

I will take my limp with stride. I am proud of my limp and will never hide it to try to give others the illusion that I walk upright. Some days that limp is more noticeable than others, and sometimes the pain from the injury is too much to bear, but I will learn to do my best with this limp for the rest of my days. My limp is a part of me, a part of my beautiful life with Sofie. Although not beautiful in the way that we had hoped, it is stunning nonetheless. And because of her beauty, I will not only learn to walk through life with this limp, but for her I will dance. I promise you this, Sofie.

When I was pregnant, naïve, and maybe even a little vain in my first life, I remember getting ready for work some mornings wondering if Sofie would think I was a fun mom, and I would wonder if she would think I was pretty as she got older. In this new life, these are things that don't matter.

Today I can guarantee you, sweet girl, that it will *not* be pretty, but I promise you Mama will keep dancing with her limp. I'll keep dancing through the pain, through any awkwardness, through the discomfort; I, baby girl, will dance for you.

I know there will be many more days ahead that are going to be daunting. It is terrifying not knowing what the future holds for us.

Will we ever be able to see little glimpses of you in any future siblings' smiles or in their eyes? Will we be able to one day tell your little sibling(s) all about their amazing big sister who captured the hearts of all who learned about her? How do we continue to find ways to parent a beautiful angel? These are things that today we do not know. But what we do know is that we are a family: Daddy, Mama, and you, our sweet angel, Sofia. You have given me the incredible gift of being your mama. What I do know is that will never change.

I may need your help many days, sweet pea, to help Mama through, to remind me to keep dancing...to keep breathing...to keep being your mama. But I promise I will honor you every day, Sofie. While not at all as we had planned, we *are* a family, and I think I am going to make it because I have a beautiful little angel on my side.

I will dance through this life that I was given, limping every step of the way. Together we'll step into this strange new world, leaving the whys, what ifs, and anger behind.

With one push, together we'll cross the threshold into a world of unknowns but also a world that is full of pure and intense love. Together our lives will be completely different because we *will* rewrite our ending, an ending full of a different kind of hope, peace, and the deepest love I will ever know. And just maybe I'll be able to see color in the world once again. Maybe I'll be able to feel joy. Maybe I'll have days where there are more smiles and less tears. Maybe I'll get there. I love you, sweet baby girl.

Each day I will breathe for her, get up for her, and just limp on. I will keep clumsily placing one feeble foot in front of the other as I stumble toward whatever lies ahead. I know she'll be there every step of the way, nudging me through gently, with just one push.

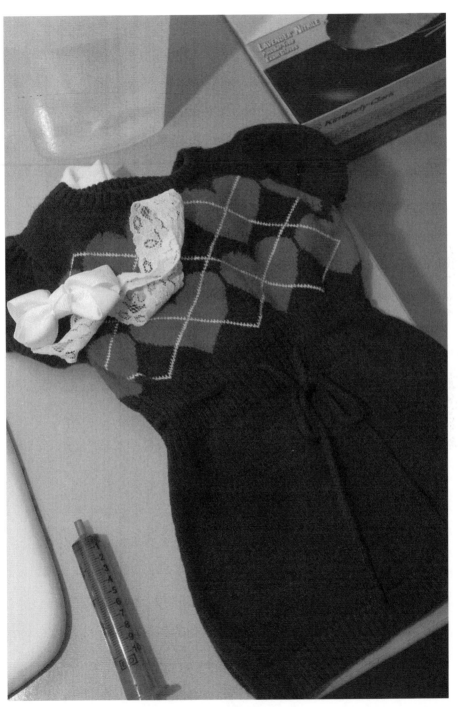

Sofie's Valentine's Day Dress.

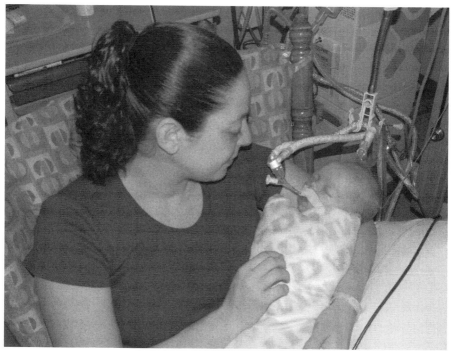

One of the first times I was able to hold Sofie.

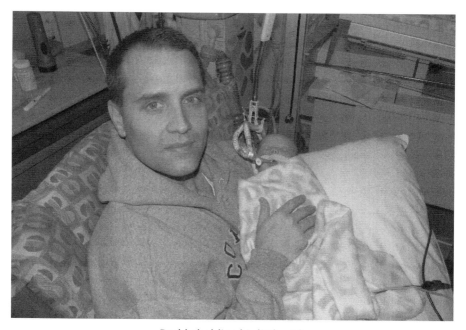

Daddy holding his little girl.

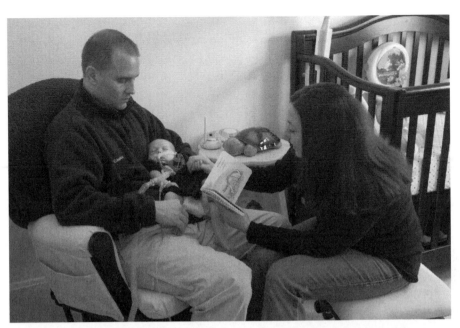

In her nursery, reading her our favorite book, for the first and last time.

If only my love could have healed her. Moments before
she was freed from her tubes.

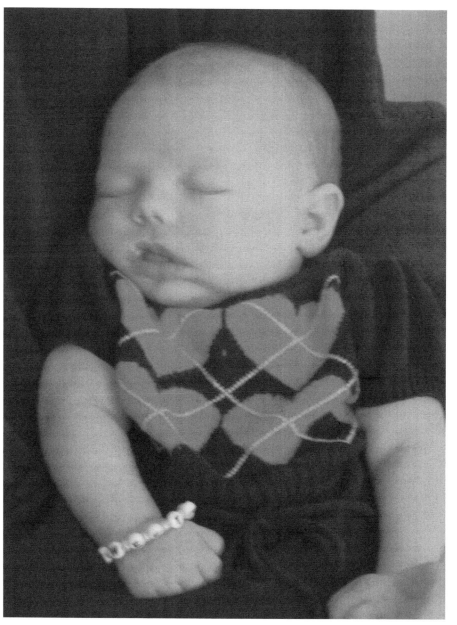

My beautiful girl, free of all tubes.

My favorite picture of Sof and her daddy.

Love.

Snuggling close as the end draws near.

Our first family photo after Sofie's little brother was born.
She is forever a part of our family.

EPILOGUE

Lori and Mike continue to reside in Ohio. In addition to her work at the local children's hospital, Lori also runs a non-profit organization that she and Mike created in honor of Sofie. Together, they continue to find ways to celebrate Sofie in their daily lives.

On August 13, 2012, Mike, Lori, and Sofia joyfully welcomed Alex to the family. Sofie's little brother, has already begun learning all about his big sister in Heaven. Her place in the family is forever honored and celebrated.

To learn more about the non-profit organization please visit teamsofiechapter2.org and see how Sofie's legacy of love continues.

Made in the USA
San Bernardino, CA
03 December 2013